AMERICAN LIBERALISM

AND IDEOLOGICAL CHANGE

AMERICAN **LIBERALISM**
AND IDEOLOGICAL CHANGE

Leonard Williams

NORTHERN ILLINOIS UNIVERSITY PRESS DEKALB 1997

© 1997 by Northern Illinois University Press
Published by the Northern Illinois University Press,
DeKalb, Illinois 60115
Manufactured in the United States
using acid-free paper ∞
All Rights Reserved
Design by Julia Fauci

Library of Congress Cataloging-in-Publication Data
Williams, Leonard A., 1952–
American liberalism and ideological change /
Leonard Williams.

   p.   cm.
Includes bibliographical references (p.   )
and index.
ISBN 0-87580-227-3 (acid-free paper)
1. Liberalism—United States—History—
20th century. 2. Opposition
(Political science)—United States—History—
20th century. 3. Political culture—United States—
History—20th century. 4. United States—Politics
and government—20th century. I. Title.
JC574.2.U6W56 1997
320.51'3'0973—dc21   96-54059
               CIP

Portions of chapter 2 first appeared in *New Political
Science.* Reprinted with permission.

Portions of chapter 4 first appeared in *The Social
Science Journal.* Reprinted with permission.

To Ruth

and to the memory of

Elaine and Jerry, Chet, and Leonard

CONTENTS

ACKNOWLEDGMENTS

At the outset I would like to thank a number of people who have made some contribution to this work. Especially notable have been those made by two former editors for Northern Illinois University Press— Daniel Coran, who provided the initial spark, and Janet Freeman, who kept the flame alive. Mary Lincoln, the director of Northern Illinois University Press, has also been both encouraging and patient in nurturing the manuscript's revision and completion. Thanks also to the anonymous reviewers who helped sharpen, clarify, and expand the argument in key places.

Because some parts of the book have been previously published in *The Social Science Journal* and in *New Political Science,* I thank those publications for permission to reprint those portions in the second and fourth chapters. Their editors and manuscript reviewers also deserve a word of appreciation for their helpful comments. Additional thanks must go to Jeanne Hickling, a tireless and resourceful reference librarian, who processed innumerable interlibrary loan requests with much good humor.

More indirect contributions were made by many colleagues and students at Manchester College, whose friendship and support, as well as intellectual and political challenges, have provided me with a remarkable atmosphere in which to work and teach. Other contributions came from three fellow social scientists—Joseph Losco, Clyde Wilcox, and Neil Wollman—each of whom has stimulated my thinking by his insistence that I pursue the merely apparent diversions of what John Stuart Mill called "other studies." I also thank Matt Hendryx for his willingness to give some last-minute advice on the crafts of writing and editing.

Finally, let no one gainsay the contributions made by my wife, Deborah, and my sons, Christopher and Jason, who have shared with me life's joys and sorrows, achievements and struggles. Without the love they have shown in countless ways, this book would be a vain and empty accomplishment.

AMERICAN LIBERALISM

AND IDEOLOGICAL CHANGE

So the paradox of political freedom, as enunciated by Jean-Jacques Rousseau, faces us in the epistemic field also. *Man is born free, and everywhere he is in chains;* yet, on closer inspection these chains turn out to be the necessary instruments of effective political freedom. Intellectually, also, Man is born with the power of original thought, and everywhere this originality is constrained within a particular conceptual inheritance; yet, on closer inspection, these concepts too turn out to be the necessary instruments of effective thought.

—Stephen Toulmin

So we have two preconditions for the fulfillment of our essential interest in leading a life that is good. One is that we lead our life from the inside, in accordance with our beliefs about what gives value to life; the other is that we be free to question those beliefs, to examine them in the light of whatever information, examples, and arguments our culture can provide.

—Will Kymlicka

CHANGING LIBERALISM

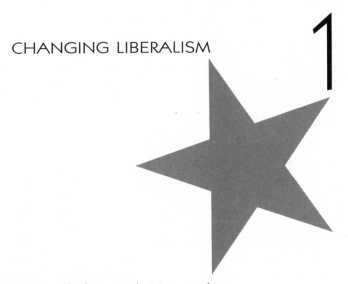

In *The German Ideology* Karl Marx and Friedrich Engels conceived of ideology as a reflexive echo or an inverted image of actual human activity. In their view, ideology and other forms of consciousness are not independent but parasitic: "They have no history, no development"; instead, by "developing their material production and their material intercourse," people "alter, along with this their real existence, their thinking and the products of their thinking" (McLellan 1977, 164). For Marx, then, changes in the domain of ideology are mere reflections of changes occurring in material life, "the real foundation" of society.

The assertion that ideological forms have no history is a puzzling one, especially for a thinker celebrated for his emphasis on the historical and developmental character of human experience. Indeed, in Marx's view the chief error of bourgeois ideology was that it made something timeless and universal out of what was historically contingent—for example, the bourgeois standpoint saw human beings as naturally self-seeking and competitive, rather than acknowledging that people appeared to be that way only in the context of capitalist society. Moreover, anyone familiar with the products of human thought (as Marx certainly was) would have to recognize that these products have been anything but static.

My purpose in this book is not to resolve the theoretical or psychological puzzle of Marx's remark. Instead, I intend to start from the premise that ideological change is simply a fact of social and political life. As many surveys of modern ideologies attest, their contemporary forms are significantly different from their original variants, even though the versions share certain family resemblances. Each of the many traditions within political or economic ideologies—liberalism, conservatism, or communism, for example—have grown and developed in various ways over the last few centuries. National circumstances and philosophical idiosyncrasies together have modified and transformed each ideological tradition. The basic fact of ideological evolution is acknowledged every time we note, say, the differences that exist between conservatism in the United States and conservatism in Europe, or between communism as it arose in Russia and communism as it developed in China. Though we have recognized the existence of ideological change, we have not done well in trying to understand it.

For all the major studies of ideology in general or of any one tradition in particular, the phenomenon of ideological change has received little sustained attention. Even a cursory reading of the literature on ideology would give one the impression that such a phenomenon either does not occur or does not matter. Indeed, we have failed to acknowledge that, for the most part, "the central research question concerning ideology becomes that of explaining why particular ideologies or ideological themes (patterns) exist in some situations and not in others—the problem that derives from assuming that ideologies are not distributed uniformly or entirely at random" (Wuthnow 1987, 148). Needless to say, the kind of concerted effort needed to explain such phenomena has not yet been exerted.

Why not? One possible reason may be that our researches have not rested on the assumption noted above. We have simply not inquired into the origins of ideology, beyond trying to locate the psychological defects that lead some people into totalitarian or millenarian pathologies. Further, the study of ideology has been hampered by our propensity to regard ideologies either as monolithic bodies of doctrine (emerging full-blown at birth and remaining static ever after) or as undergoing such subtle modifications that only devotees of nuance need to be concerned.

Yet even though we *treat* ideologies as static phenomena, we all *know* that significant ideological changes do indeed occur. The diverse currents and doctrinal shifts found in the history of Marxism are nothing if not examples of the phenomenon. Another prime example can be found in British political thought, with its shift from the laissez-faire strictures of Social Darwinism to the ameliorative concerns of a new liberalism (Van Dyke 1995, 13–24). Such changes need to be explained; they cannot be taken for granted or treated merely as natural occurrences. Assuredly, the contemporary troubles our political traditions face suggest that ideological change must not only be explained; for some observers, it must also be promoted.

TAKING POLEMICS SERIOUSLY

Liberalism is in crisis. The most enduring public philosophy of our age has been criticized, defended, reconsidered, and by some, dismissed. Many ideological movements have emerged in the course of this crisis and have offered new visions of society and politics. In response, political and social theorists have tried to trace a reconstituted public philosophy that would either bolster or replace our liberal heritage.

The contemporary crisis of American liberalism has thus stimulated a great deal of discussion and theoretical work. Modern liberals have been attacked by innumerable critics for a host of sins. For example, in the realm of practice, radicals on both the Right and the Left have accused liberals of waffling on significant moral issues and of creating an overgrown bureaucratic state, run for the benefit of organized interest groups (so-called special interests) or of political and intellectual elites (said to constitute a "new class"). Both the friends and the enemies of liberalism have noted still other symptoms of its crisis: the failure of and disenchantment with Great Society–era social programs, widespread agreement among observers and activists alike that "the era of big government is over," and the dissolution of the Democratic party's electoral coalition.

In a more theoretical vein, political philosophers have been prompted by the crisis to criticize the entire liberal tradition—both modern and classical liberalism—for its weak epistemological grounding, its suspect assumptions, and its problematic values. In response to the challenges raised, political theorists have adopted several strategies (Dunn 1985; Pennock 1990; Terchek 1986). One approach has defended liberalism against attacks from various ideological quarters—namely, conservatism, traditionalism, communitarianism, Marxism, and more recently, feminism. This strategy has involved showing that (because of its open-ended, nondogmatic character) the liberal tradition simply has not merited the scorn heaped upon it.

Another approach has explored the philosophical bases, the ontological assumptions, that liberals of all stripes either do or ought to share. It has sought to prove that liberalism is a doctrine that demands the assent of rational people and to show that the philosophical foundations of liberalism are, in the final analysis, not in disrepair. A third response has nevertheless conceded that liberal political thought and action has indeed fallen on hard times. In other words, contemporary liberalism faces difficulties that will be surmounted only if it can somehow be reconstructed. Thus, liberalism must acknowledge its limitations, be put on a firmer foundation, and acquire a new conceptual apparatus, if it is to survive.

The trouble with these responses is that none of them truly addresses the political context in which the contemporary crisis of liberalism has occurred. Obviously, recent decades have presented us with neither the first nor the only time of trouble for liberal political thought. Liberalism as an ideology or a philosophical tradition may be particularly, even inherently, prone to crisis (Cumming 1969). Political observers in several eras in American history either have perceived a crisis in liberal orthodoxy or have tried to provoke liberalism into one. The point here, though, is not to suggest that American liberalism's most recent predicament is somehow *sui generis* but rather to observe that many of our responses to it have been marked by political theory's well-documented alienation from actual political concerns (Barber 1988; Fowler 1983; Gunnell 1986; Kress 1983).

Despite all the discussion and attention given to liberalism in contemporary political theory, current debates have largely neglected what may well be a central point of the theoretical enterprise. Academic debates about liberalism frequently have focused upon such abstract philosophical questions as the nature of the self, the standpoints of neutrality or rationality, and the meaning of concepts such as justice and right (Wallach 1987). Yet in very few of the discussions does one get a clear sense of what political stakes are being fought over.

Many treatments of the crisis of liberalism thus have been altogether too alienated from the everyday practice of politics, whether in thought or in action. An alienated political theory is one that forgets the admonition of Paul Ricoeur that politics is not a science but, rather, "an art of orienting oneself among conflicting groups. The concept of politics must remain polemical; there is a place for polemics in life, and to acknowledge this is the honest import of the problem" (1981, 179). For political theory to end its alienated condition requires, I believe, that political theorists begin to take polemics seriously.

Taking polemics seriously means, initially, that we acknowledge that

> politics remains something human beings *do*, not something they possess or use or watch or talk or think about. Those who would do something about it must do more than philosophize, and philosophy that is politically intelligible must take the full political measure of politics as conduct. (Barber 1988, 11, original emphasis)

To make theoretical debates over liberalism "politically intelligible" therefore requires moving away from abstract philosophical concerns and toward more concrete political ones. In particular, one prime political concern has to do with the process of reconstructing liberalism to meet the needs and social facts of the present era; a process that requires both promoting and understanding the phenomenon of ideological change.

Political theorists thus need to focus not merely on the elaboration and defense of liberal philosophical foundations, but also on the goal of overcoming the current ideological crisis. Discussions of liberal theory or principles must therefore be conjoined with understandings of contemporary economic, social, and political constellations. David Paris has suggested two ways by which this result could be achieved: either through "an ethnographic approach that examines the various ways in which principles are understood" (e.g., using public opinion surveys, depth interviews, or philosophical analyses to explore liberal concepts and principles), or through examining liberal commitments "in light of the details of a specific policy or policy area" (1987, 935).

An alternative strategy, I believe, starts with the suggestion that political theorists focus on the idea (or rather, the practice) of ideological reconstruction, on what it might take to articulate and justify a new variant of liberalism. We need to show what a new liberalism might look like in the current context. This is not an easy task, since (as Hegel reminds us) our grasp of the present is rather tenuous, especially when compared to our ability to reconstruct and understand the past. Nor is it an easy task to perform in the cultural context of the United States, which is commonly regarded as having a uniquely nonideological form of politics. This is not to say that ideas have not been employed by political thinkers and activists, but it is to say, with Michael Foley, that "there is a rich store of alternative ideas—or rather of alternative constructions, meanings and usages of ideas—in American politics" (1991, 125). At the very least, we can analyze and assess the efforts of those who have undertaken the task of ideological reconstruction.

In doing so, we recognize that philosophers and theorists do not have a monopoly on serious thinking about politics. All too often, though, the pundit or the polemicist is dismissed by academic theorists as unworthy of their attention. Just as the bane of the natural or social scientist has been the popularizer or the journalist, so the polemicist similarly has perturbed the political or social theorist. Even when studying an ideology or a public philosophy (seen as action-oriented ideas or the operative ideals underlying public policy), political theorists have largely preferred to focus on the works of other theorists. Few of us have tried to grapple with the raw, truncated, even unfinished theories implicit in everyday political argument.

Clearly, we have little reason to expect the likes of E. J. Dionne, Jr., or George Will, Robert Reich or Newt Gingrich, to exhibit the sort of conceptual precision, theoretical coherence, tight argumentation, or even sheer brilliance, that we find in the classic works of political and social philosophers. If the thirty-second political advertisements that mark our election campaigns today may be seen as "the haiku of political thought," we might regard the fully developed political theories of philosophers and academics as akin to novels and contrast them with the ideas of the polemicists, now perhaps seen as the lyric poetry of political thought (Biocca 1991, xi). Still, polemics present us with a rather special sort of poetry, for (as has been underscored by recent debates over the canon and other cultural objects) there is a very real sense in which both academic and political arguments may be viewed as analogous to war (Gergen 1994).

The end result of these considerations, I think, is that political theorists have to set aside (at least for a moment) their usual tendency to address issues with the intent of resolving confusions about them. Instead, we must turn our attention to the ways in which ideas have been both the symptoms and the weapons of political conflict. Perhaps, as one recent examination of narrative and discourse in American politics has suggested, the preferred approach should be to explore "theses not to prove or disprove them but to discover the consequences of entertaining them" (Dolan 1994, 11).

Taking polemics seriously, then, requires that political theorists attend to different sources of political ideas than many are used to consulting. It means that some of our theoretical goals must shift as well. Even so, we need not abandon everything we now do. The arguments and claims of standard political and social theorists cannot be neglected. Nor should we entirely forget the interests and activities traditionally associated with the theoretical enterprise. When scholars have examined the course of philosophical controversies, for example, they have sometimes spoken of and explored theoretical interventions or various moves in an argument. In other words, they have implicitly acknowledged a connection between theory and behavior, between discursive practices and political games.

The intent of this book, though, is not to provide definitive treatments of specific ideological conflicts. I do not wish to give a play-by-play account of contemporary quarrels or to keep score for one or another side of partisans. Nor have I sought to present a reconstructed liberalism that solves either the political problems faced by its modern variant or the philosophical problems faced by the liberal tradition itself. My approach does not involve arguing with the claims made by various theorists nor resolving in a more or less final sense any particular practical disputes. Instead, my goal has been to observe theoretical behavior, to log and describe actions taken in the realm of consciousness—actions aimed at reforming or altering that consciousness itself. In short, the ideological positions described herein are treated as categories, and the theoretical moves made by their adherents become data for an investigation into the phenomenon of ideological change.

AMERICAN LIBERALISM

Regardless of the approach we take in understanding and addressing liberalism's current crisis, clearly the time is ripe for a reconsideration of the grand tradition of American political thought—for many, a decidedly liberal tradition. Of course, any attempt to do so must come to terms with the lengthy shadow cast by the foundational work of Louis Hartz (1955), which saw our political tradition as an early embrace of and, thereafter, the steady development of Lockean liberalism. Hartz used the Tocquevillean insight that Americans were "born equal," that we lacked a feudal tradition, to explain the absence from our political scene of both a traditionalist conservatism and an authentic socialism. In an era of consensus and complacency, Hartz's work provided one of the more noteworthy examples of studies by historians and social scientists that regarded the United States as a sort of utopia where political conflict was restricted to means rather than ends (Bell 1960; Boorstin 1953; Lipset 1963).

Some decades later, in the quiet aftermath of the social and political upheaval that marked the 1960s, Samuel Huntington (1981) and Lawrence Herson (1984) reemphasized the American tradition's fundamental continuity. They argued that the "American political creed" (with its host of basic values such as liberty, equality, achievement, property, localism, and democracy) accounts for both liberalism's pervasive hold on our minds and our policies, and the occasional rebellions that occur when our politics fails to live up to its ideals. In this view, paradoxically, our "widespread consensus on liberal democratic values provides the basis for challenging the legitimacy of American political practices and the authority of American political institutions" (Huntington 1981, 32). From time to time the gap between those practices and our ideals produces political discontent, the rise of social movements, and intense calls for institutional reform. These periods of "creedal passion," though, ultimately yield little more than the reinvocation and the reaffirmation of the consensual creed. Thus, while acknowledging significant episodes of political conflict, some studies nevertheless returned (quite reassuringly) to a vision of the American political tradition as, if not monolithic, then at least monovocal.

Consensus-oriented approaches to understanding American political ideas have more recently been replaced by works that challenge the prevailing scholarly images of our political culture. For some students of American politics, the unitary vision advanced by Hartz has given way to a more binary one in which the dominant liberal tradition alternates with an equally compelling competitor, whether Christian or civic republican. American political thought is thus no longer marked by the unchallenged dominance of Lockean liberalism. Instead, our tradition is now characterized by an essential tension.

Quite a number of historians and political theorists have embraced this more dialectical conception of the American political tradition, especially since Bernard Bailyn (1967) and Gordon Wood (1969) found that a spirit of republican virtue animated the politics of the colonial and revolutionary periods. One puzzle for some scholars of political thought thus centered on what became of that spirit after the ratification of the Constitution. For John Diggins (1984), the solution lay in the discovery that the rhetoric of virtue found in the revolutionary period was more liberal (emphasizing negative freedom) than republican (focused on community). Though themes of consensus and continuity remain in Diggins's account, it nonetheless posits (contrary to Hartz) a significant alternative to liberalism and its privatized pursuit of passion and interest—an alternative found in the generally neglected, largely Calvinist, religious convictions of such figures as John Locke and Abraham Lincoln.

In the eyes of Diggins, those convictions ultimately represented one of "two incompatible value systems struggling for the soul of America: the liberal idea of labor, competition, and self-help and the Christian idea of sin, atonement, and redemption" (1984, 326). In a similar vein, H. Mark Roelofs has observed that our political culture suffers from the paradox of wanting "to be both an egalitarian, community-loving social democracy seeking broad goals of social justice, and, at the same time, a freedom-loving, privatistic, interest-seeking liberal democracy with powerfully sustained elitist tendencies" (1992, 1). The alternation between liberal and Calvinist values, between Protestant and bourgeois cultures, found by these scholars also has its parallel in a similar pattern of alternation between Hamiltonian and Jeffersonian ideas identified by Kenneth Dolbeare and Linda Medcalf (1988).

Though liberalism in these accounts remains our dominant tradition, still other students of American politics have asserted that the civic republicanism that characterized the revolutionary period never really went away. As a strain of thought whose predecessors include Machiavelli and Aristotle, republicanism has long remained an attractive counterpoint to Enlightenment liberalism (Pocock 1975; Sullivan 1986). Not only has it provided a philosophical alternative to liberalism; the "democratic wish" that characterizes the republican tradition has actually shaped the practice of American politics during a few critical periods of reform. In such periods liberal emphases on "individuals, representation . . . , private interest, and individualism" give way, however briefly, to republican themes of "the people, participation, common good, and community" (Morone 1990, 8).

There are two difficulties with such narratives of American liberalism, though. One is that they presume that an alternative tradition (such as republicanism) has had the same degree of coherence and the same degree of adherence as liberalism. Had this been the case, obviously, the Hartz thesis would have been much less plausible; even though it is subject to criticism, few doubt that liberalism has been the dominant ideology in the United States. That dominant position cannot and should not be obscured by claims of an enduring republican counterpoint. Indeed, as David Plotke suggests, those claims become much "more persuasive if recast as claims about republican motifs within a liberal framework" (1996, 17).

The second, and more significant, difficulty centers on the assumption by these accounts that there is a permanent dualism between traditions. In this well-choreographed, theoretical pas de deux, liberalism is forever faced with recurrent challenges from a single subordinate ideological tradition. Rather than meeting opponents arguing from any of several alternative positions, liberalism in this account plays the bourgeoisie to Calvinism's or republicanism's proletariat. Fortunately, though, some historians and political theorists have begun to take issue with this assumption and to avoid the dramatic essentialism it represents.

Philip Abbott's intriguing look (1980) at the political thought of "post-liberals" provides a case in point. Though their attacks have varied, these authors have shared the belief that not only does American liberalism suffer from serious inadequacies in both theory and policy, but it is also difficult to find any special coherence in liberal ideology. Indeed, Abbott has suggested that, for the reader following his survey of postliberal thinkers, the history of American liberalism gradually unravels to reveal not one, but four varieties of liberal thought—welfare, scientific, pluralist, and utopian liberalism (1980, 14–24).

Rather than being a monolithic culture of Lockean conformity, "the United States has in reality the bright colours of several political traditions, usually held together in a loose weave, but often coming apart and providing the occasion for a conflict of fundamental ideas and principles," according to Michael Foley (1991, 5). The assertion that our political tradition is actually a set of multiple traditions has also been supported by Rogers Smith (1993) and James Young (1996). In their eyes, American political thought is filled with too much ambiguity and complexity for the simple story of consensus and continuity to be swallowed whole, without any qualification or amendment.

Finally, Richard Ellis (1993) has employed the cultural theory of Aaron Wildavsky and Mary Douglas to identify not one, not two, but five distinct cultural strains in our history. Many of the policy disputes the nation has encountered, many of its enduring value-oriented debates, can be traced to the rival understandings of human needs and purposes respectively put forward by the cultures Ellis has discovered— individualism, egalitarianism, hierarchy, fatalism, and hermitude. Though five cultures may be found, he nonetheless believes that only the first two have any significant roots in what we commonly describe as liberalism. Thus, from his assertion of multiple traditions, Ellis returns to the familiar dualism and concludes that any "satisfactory theory of American political cultures must acknowledge both the pervasive individualism of American life and the centrality of the communitarian or egalitarian challenge" (1993, 154).

In the shadow of Louis Hartz, then, synoptic views of the American political tradition have begun to move away from the sort of consensus once said to mark the tradition itself. New interpretations of that tradition suggest that the American public philosophy is not entirely consensual or unitary but, rather, that it contains at least two (and perhaps more) relatively independent strands of thought. At this point, though, it is probably impossible to try to discover the fact of the matter concerning the essential nature of the American political tradition. Scholars in the pro-Hartz camp, no doubt, will continue to find evidence of a continuously dominant liberalism, whereas their critics should have little trouble producing equally convincing evidence of a more plurivocal tradition. Without having to take sides, it requires but a moment's reflection to realize that we do indeed have a "little understood ability to engage in deep conflicts over political ideas, while at the same time reducing the adversarial positions to legitimate derivatives of American history and development" (Foley 1991, 4).

Nonetheless, we should be mindful that the American version is not the only liberalism that encompasses a seeming multitude of ideas. Anthony Arblaster (1984), for example, has made special note of the fact that in England liberal ideas (especially those resulting from an individualistic heritage) are so pervasive that they can be shared comfortably by both conservatives and social democrats. Indeed, in many ways, liberalism's all-embracing character is the source of both its strengths and its weaknesses as a political outlook. Containing both radical and conservative elements, "in nineteenth-century England, liberalism as a theoretical expression of social life supplied the values, assumptions, and arguments for both a defense and a radical critique of the existing social order" (Ashcraft 1993, 249).

Given such a nonunitary tradition, it is only natural that recombinatory efforts should occur from time to time. Indeed, both Arblaster and

Vernon Van Dyke (1995) highlight the efforts at ideological reconstruction that occurred within British liberalism at the turn of the century. My goal in this book is to understand what forms similar efforts have taken in the American context and to explore theoretically the nature of ideological change. For our purposes, then, it makes little difference whether the Lockean monolith has stood firm like Gibraltar, eroded like Stonehenge, or been dismantled like the Berlin Wall. What does matter is that American liberalism no longer appears as uniform as it once did.

This suggests that our study must proceed using an assumption different from the one that has governed previous work. We must assume that any given philosophical or ideological tradition is rarely monolithic or unidirectional; rather, it most likely contains a number of coexisting strains that can be drawn upon as the needs of the moment require. This assumption is not unwarranted, especially when we consider the practical demands placed upon any tradition of thought and action. Stanley Fish, for example, notes that the activity of reading literary texts occurs within disciplinary routines "that are at once open, in that they accommodate themselves to novelty, and closed, in that the aftermath of accommodation is a reconfiguration and not an elimination of a disciplinary boundary" (1995, 48–49). Like Fishian criticism, so Kuhnian science and Wittgensteinian practices. Ideological traditions similarly face demands both to accommodate novelty and to maintain their identity and thus are simultaneously pluri- and monovocal.

IDEOLOGY AND IDEOLOGICAL CHANGE

As we all know, *ideology* is one of the most curious concepts in the social sciences—a concept as disparaged as it is indispensable. For both social scientists and average citizens, ideology has long been regarded as the domain of the extremist, the tool of the totalitarian revolutionary. Ideological modes of thought have been identified as at least closed-minded, if not completely delusional. So much is ideology derided that, from time to time, we announce the "end of ideology," a glorious era in which we can set aside our differences over fundamental values and bask in the glow of self-assured consensus.

As soon as the latest end of ideology is announced, though, it reappears with increasing vigor. No sooner had Daniel Bell (1960) proclaimed "the exhaustion of political ideas" in the 1950s, than the political and ideological movements of the 1960s emerged to belie his claims. More recently, the rise of Islamic and Christian fundamentalism, the reemergence of nationalism and terrorism, as well as the occasional "battle for the soul" of major American political parties, have all underscored the continuing significance of ideological phenomena.

But ideology is important not only for its persistence. We have to acknowledge that it remains the primary means by which people relate to political life. It provides the lenses through which we view political events, the conceptual framework through which we come to understand the political world we inhabit. Similarly, ideology provides us with a set of standards by which to evaluate the social and political order in which we live; it gives us a set of values and helps us construct a vision of a better society. Finally, an ideology will tell us how we should act in public affairs, what we should do (if anything) to bring our society more in line with our utopian vision. In brief, an ideology is simply a practical political theory (Ball and Dagger 1991, 8–12; Dolbeare and Dolbeare 1976, 5–11).

Conceived in this way, ideology is an essential part of modern political life. It seems that we can no more do without ideology than we can do without breathing. In American politics, nonetheless, we frequently claim to be nonideological, and we generally laud politicians who are pragmatic or "middle-of-the-road." By this we mean simply that we prefer a politics that is open-minded and open-ended. Ideology is not banished from our politics, though, for all our perspectives on politics, all our belief systems, can be regarded as more or less systematically developed ideologies. Everyone has an ideology.

Yet, my focus here will not be on mapping the cognitive structures of a representative set of individuals. That is certainly a worthwhile endeavor, but this book is more about what Robert Lane called "forensic" or "manifest" ideology, that is, the complex belief systems articulated by political theorists and activists (1962). Even in this context, it is still a mistake to define ideology too narrowly as a comprehensive program of action or as a totalizing, if not totalitarian, belief system. As Martin Seliger (1976) has observed, to define ideology either as the belief system of one's opponents or as the closed-mindedness of the stereotypical ideologue is to overlook broader social and political phenomena that also go by the name of ideology.

As used here, ideology will refer (at least in part) to what somewhat old-fashioned folks refer to as *isms*—those philosophical and cultural traditions that have shaped and animated regimes and movements. Another synonym for my broad use of the term would be *public philosophy*—the operative ideals that underlie the institutions and practices of political life, the understandings about politics and society that a people share (Lowi 1979; Sullivan 1986). Still another synonym may be found in the term *discourse,* which highlights not only shared meanings and concepts, but also the institutionally embedded character of thoughts about politics and policies (Plotke 1996; Thompson 1984). We need not offer at this point a universally acceptable, comprehensive definition of the concept of ideology. That goal has eluded many a social scientist and political theorist, and it would certainly elude me as well. Instead, relying upon general intuitions and understandings of the term, I intend to work within an area of ideology theory that has so far been left underdeveloped, if it has not gone entirely unexplored.

Here, then, is an unresolved problem facing any coherent theory of ideology or political culture: How do ideologies (specifically, ideological traditions or public philosophies such as liberalism or conservatism) change? Before that question can be answered, some preliminary discussion of ideology theory (how we understand the concept and phenomenon of ideology) is necessary. So, in chapter 2 I explore two contemporary approaches to understanding the nature of ideology—namely, that of Marxist theory and that of hermeneutics or interpretation. The first approach treats ideology as an unhealthy and exogenous, if not altogether alien, factor in political and social life. At the same time, to the extent that an ideological orthodoxy cannot be overthrown through revolutionary upheaval or the triumph of Marxist science, it permeates all political thought and action. The second regards ideological phenomena as endemic to political and social life, and so, rather than being read out of existence by an opposing force from outside, ideology has to be understood as a cultural phenomenon and, like any text, criticized immanently. From there, in chapters 3, 4, and 5, I explore how the standpoint of immanent critique can help us understand ideological change.

In these chapters I consider significant modes of argument that have affected the evolution of modern American liberalism, that is, arguments associated with periods marked by Progressivism and the rise of New Deal liberalism, with the political upheaval and oppositional politics of the 1960s and beyond, and with various efforts to reconstruct liberalism in the 1980s and 1990s. In particular, in chapter 3 I show

how both reform liberals and neoliberals (personified by John Dewey and Robert Reich, respectively) have conceived of ideological change as a process requiring a full-fledged cultural transformation. In chapter 4 efforts at ideological change appear in the guise of frontal assaults on the liberal tradition, and so I look at the patterns of oppositional politics shaped by the New Left and the New Right. Then, in chapter 5, I examine both communitarian and feminist efforts to change liberalism by means of philosophical critiques of its fundamental concepts.

In these intermediate chapters, my goal is not to solve social problems or resolve theoretical disagreements, but merely to highlight certain tendencies and strategies of argument. Each of these chapters focuses on some exemplary efforts to challenge and transform American liberalism through cultural transformation, oppositional politics, or conceptual critique. Typically, of course, those arguments for ideological change are somewhat interconnected. For example, as Dewey's work itself shows, it is hard to imagine a call for cultural transformation that does not also include some revision of generally accepted conceptual understandings. Moreover, the people and movements chosen as exemplars of a particular style of argument also could have been used to illustrate one of the other approaches. Nonetheless, despite some interconnections and overlaps, the discussion in each of the three chapters will be confined to a single approach.

After examining the arguments put forward in debates about the fate of American liberalism, several theories about change in social and intellectual life are surveyed and the merits of aproaches to effecting ideological change are assessed. Among the conclusions presented in chapter 6 is the central idea that ideological change is a multifaceted and complex, incremental and not wholly rational affair. Faced with what I call the "dilemma of congruence," people who seek to transform or replace a dominant ideological orthodoxy are most likely to do so by resurrecting submerged or marginalized elements of its tradition.

What I have sought to do in this book is to examine the phenomenon of change in one particular ideology (liberalism), for a relatively short span of time (from about the 1930s to the present), and in a single political and cultural location (the United States). Since the United States has long been regarded as a nonideological society, the existence of *any* ideological change here should, of course, be a phenomenon worthy of note and even more worthy of examination. Further, since American political thought has been shaped by an especially dominant liberal consensus, efforts to alter or undermine that consensus may well be as revealing as they have been poignant.

As popular dissatisfaction and philosophical discontent with American liberalism have arisen, pressures for political change have mounted. Fundamental political change, though, first requires changing our dominant ideology, our public philosophy, our political consciousness, even our very ideas about change. I seek here, then, to see how ideological change has been argued for, and thereby to gain some insight into how such change may be achieved. I also hope to provide a stimulus for developing a theory of ideological change that accords with both an understanding of the dynamics of change and an appreciation for the vicissitudes of American liberalism.

INTERPRETATION, CRITIQUE,
AND THE PROBLEM OF
IDEOLOGICAL CHANGE

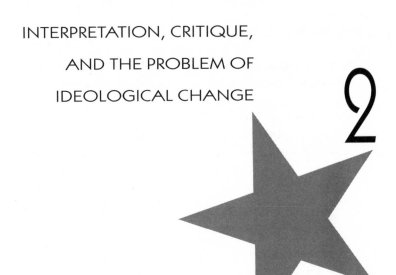

2

Without a doubt, as chapter 1 suggests, the development of American liberalism must now be seen as more complex than it first appeared to be. Previously having viewed our political tradition as the continuous evolution of Lockeanism, we now see it as a dialectical tension between alternative traditions (liberal versus Calvinist, or liberal versus republican), if not as a more manifold set of competing orientations. A similar complexity marks the concept of ideology, with its diverse meanings and conceptions in both Marxist and non-Marxist traditions (Goldie 1989; Larrain 1983; McLellan 1995; Seliger 1976). Though the concept cannot be wholly divorced from its polemical or critical connotations, we now find it difficult to regard ideology as simple error, illusion, or distortion. It is not solely the province of the extremist, nor does it denote a set of beliefs held by captives of superstition or by unsophisticated folk who lack scientific knowledge.

Ideology thus remains an important concept for social theory. We find it difficult to discuss modern politics without using ideological labels or discourse—without referring to liberals or conservatives, socialists or fundamentalists. So we must still face the question of how to understand the nature of ideology. The simple fact is that one cannot conceive of a society without an ideology; it is the glue that holds a society together. Similarly, one cannot conceive of an individual without an ideology; one must have at least a rudimentary belief system if one is to function as a human being in society.

If every society and every individual may be said to have an ideology, one important theoretical task is to identify and understand any society's ideological orthodoxy and its alternatives. The theorist both analyzes and interprets social structures and patterns of belief, as well as their interactions. An adequate theory of ideology has to be both hermeneutic and critical; it must understand ideology and link it with such related concepts as power and domination (McLellan 1995, 83). The extent to which the path of interpretation can also be a path of critique has long been at issue—a matter of importance not only to theorists, but also to activists seeking to transform the way we see the world. In this chapter I explore the relevance of that controversy for the theory of ideology and ideological change.

READING AND INTERPRETATION

Among the many theorists who have focused on ideology, none has been more noteworthy or more provocative than Louis Althusser. In the thirty or so years since Althusser's essays first appeared, a great deal has been written on his theory of ideology, especially within radical intellectual circles (see, for example, Eagleton 1991; Gane 1983; Hall 1985; Hirst 1976; Rancière 1974; Therborn 1980). Despite the continuing importance of both the phenomenon and the concept of ideology to social and political life, his work on this topic generally has been ignored by more mainstream social and political theorists, with only a few exceptions (James 1985; Ricoeur 1986; Williams 1993). As the concept of ideology regains its salience, political theorists should perhaps reconsider a thinker who did much to give the concept renewed visibility.

One of Althusser's contributions to Marxism in general, and to ideology theory in particular, has been to direct our attention to the demands of discourse analysis, to the importance of "readings." For Althusser, both Marx and Freud provide examples of useful approaches to understanding texts and text analogs. In his critique of classical political economy, for example, Marx both catalogs its omissions and shows that those omissions were essential to its very nature. Similarly, Freud's analysis of parapraxes and dreams discovers that otherwise innocent speech and thinking serves as a cover for the language of the unconscious.

To follow these exemplars is to subject every text first to a surface reading and then to a depth interpretation. The second, or symptomatic, reading "divulges the undivulged event in the text it reads, and in the same movement relates it to a *different text,* present as a necessary absence in the first" (Althusser and Balibar 1970, 28, original emphasis). A symptomatic reading focuses on what is underneath or behind the words of a text, that is, on the silences, absences, omissions, errors, and contradictions that are nonetheless necessary components of the text.

Though symptomatic readings are most likely given for the texts of one's political opponents (there are, after all, no "innocent" readings), Althusser uses this approach primarily in his celebrated "return to Marx" in order to illuminate the underlying philosophy that either Marx left unexpressed or others who followed him mangled. The only difficulty is that Marx's corpus, like that of any other significant thinker, is more opaque than transparent. Revealing the essential features of his philosophy therefore requires "the application of Marxist theory to Marx himself" (Althusser 1969, 38).

The end result of Althusser's reading was, of course, the periodization of Marx's corpus by means of the concept of an epistemological break. The young Marx and the early works before the break (prior to 1845) are simply not the whole of Marx; indeed, strictly speaking, they are not even Marxist. One should note here, though, that the concept of the break itself is given a different treatment on either end of an apparent "break" in Althusser's own work. First advanced in *For Marx,* the epistemological break in Marx's work is later acknowledged to have been incomplete and to have been erroneously labeled as a philosophical, as well as a scientific, break (Althusser 1969, 34–35 and 1976, 66–72).

Nevertheless, to understand the nature of Marx's epistemological break, Althusser applies a Marxist (or, perhaps, Althusserian) theory of ideological development focused upon three basic principles: (1) Ideologies are unitary wholes; they do not consist of individual elements that can be extracted or altered without also affecting the whole. (2) Ideologies are unified by a problematic, by a set of problems and solutions, questions and answers. (3) Ideologies develop out of the relationship between an individual author and history; they constitute answers to questions posed not merely by the ideologue but also by the times, by his or her society (Althusser 1969, 62–63). By applying these principles,

Althusser suggests that Marx does not merely invert Hegel, but instead transforms the problematic; that is, Marx retreats from the domain of ideology (Hegelianism or humanism) and returns to the domain of real individuals in real history.

For Althusser, then, the influence of ideology can be found in the silences of a text and thus can be discovered only through a symptomatic reading of that text. As a result, Althusser reads Marx's works not from a chronological viewpoint, but from the perspective of a fully developed (Althusserian) Marxism. The texts in which Marx presents an authentic science thus can be effectively distinguished from those in which he articulates a humanist, Hegelian ideology.

When Paul Ricoeur turned his attention to the theory of ideology, he sought to understand Marx's corpus by applying a more hermeneutic approach. In contrast to the teleological approach of Althusser, Ricoeur's approach to reading (1981 and 1986) is decidedly more developmental or genetic. Whereas Althusser starts with a textual phenomenon at its maturity and then accounts for its inevitability in light of that end, Ricoeur starts with a text's origins and then shows the continuity of later stages with earlier ones. Ricoeur thus opposes Althusser's rejection of the young Marx, and he notes that if there was an epistemological break in Marx's work, it was not a move from science to humanism, but a transition from an inauthentic humanism to an authentic one. In many respects Althusser's teleological, even Whiggish, approach simply obscures the fact that different works have different scopes and concepts and hence serve very different purposes.

Although I think this is precisely the point of Althusser's concept of the break, Ricoeur suggests that a wholly structuralist approach to reading is sorely misguided. The problem with structuralism is that its view of reading sees the text as essentially closed upon itself, leaving the reader with little to do but inventory a discourse's elements, array them in opposition to one another, and then develop the appropriate combinatory (Ricoeur 1974a, 79). Structuralism thus makes interpretation a kind of linguistic determinism in which an author or speaker is subject to a severe set of constraints on what may be thought or said. So conceived, a given discourse lacks any transcendent aim, any intentional effort at communication. It is no wonder, then, that under a structuralist interpretation a text quite easily becomes a subjectless, contextless, easily manipulable set of units.

Ricoeur's own approach to reading acknowledges that a text will have its own scope and concept and will always point to a world beyond it. His approach begins with an explicit recognition of a text or a discourse's open character. For Ricoeur, any discourse has both a subject and a reference; in it someone says something about something to someone. Thus, the language of discourse opens out onto the world (Ricoeur 1974a, 87–88). This open character is further ensured by the process of *distanciation,* in which a text takes on a life of its own and becomes separated from its intended meaning.

As a result of distanciation, "what the text says now matters more than what the author meant to say, and every exegesis unfolds its procedures within the circumference of a meaning that has broken its moorings to the psychology of its author" (Ricoeur 1981, 201). Just as the author's intended meaning is no longer available, so the intended audience disappears as it enlarges to become the universe of all potential readers. Further, since the objectified text cannot be queried for clarification, interpretation becomes a process of creating meaning rather than simply discovering it. In the process of understanding the text, one begins to understand oneself as well.

Significantly, Ricoeur does not jettison structural analysis entirely, but instead regards it as a necessary stage between a naive, surface interpretation and a critical, depth one. At that first stage, though, structuralism must still be supplemented by hermeneutics. This is so because the very elements of discourse (words, sentences, and texts) are polysemic, ambiguous, and plurivocal; they have a multitude of possible meanings across determinate contexts. Thus, the interpretation of any text, the construction of its meaning, will always be an openended process of rational argumentation and debate (Ricoeur 1981, 161, 175–76).

Interpretation, for Ricoeur, is neither a matter of unearthing an overt or unconscious fact nor one of empirical analysis, but rather involves both orientation and projection. As a matter of orientation, every reading will inevitably be theory-laden. In order to interpret a work, a reader must necessarily locate himself or herself within a community or a tradition of thought—a location and a process that underscore the open-ended character of discourse. As a matter of projection, too, any process of reading will thus have a transcendent character, for understanding a text "is not to find a lifeless sense which is contained therein, but to unfold the possibility of being indicated by the text" (Ricoeur 1981, 56).

CONCEPTIONS OF IDEOLOGY

Despite their differences, Althusser's famous slogan that "there is no such thing as an innocent reading" (1971, 15) can be readily paired with Ricoeur's observation that every reading occurs "within a community, a tradition, or a living current of thought, all of which display presuppositions and exigencies" (1974a, 3). This agreement that the interpretation of any text or discourse is necessarily theory-laden has a parallel in Althusser's and Ricoeur's respective conceptions of ideology. Both have moved away from negative and toward positive views of what constitutes an ideology.

For example, in the course of his reading of Marx, Althusser offers several different conceptions of ideology. Althusser's discussion of Marx's epistemological break, his focus on a sort of philosophy of science, led to the first conception of ideology as a system of representations "distinguished from science in that in it the practico-social function [reproducing social relations] is more important than the theoretical function (function as knowledge)" (Althusser 1969, 231). Ideologies thus constitute broad, amorphous, and errant understandings of the world; they are mythlike precursors of authentic science. Only a scientific perspective, then, offers the prospect of escaping from the grips of ideology.

A second conception advanced by Althusser regards ideology as the lived relation of people with the world (Althusser 1969, 234). By virtue of their "imaginary" character, ideologies sometimes appear as expressions of will or desire, as wish fulfillments. Yet, because an ideology is a *lived* relation, it cannot be dismissed as being merely false, distorted, or illusory. Ideological representations of reality are found in nearly all aspects of social life. We find ideology in our beliefs and attitudes about work, family, economics, politics, nature, and organizations. Thus, ideologies do express some kind of truth, truth about the lived experience of individuals in such regions of life as religion, politics, philosophy, morality, and aesthetics.

Not all representations of that lived experience, though, are necessarily adequate or correct. Ideological representations are inadequate, spontaneous, or uncritical; they misrecognize one's real conditions of existence by denying the existence of the contradictions of life in a given mode of production. For Althusser, as for Marx, an ideology is not simply an illusion or a false consciousness, but a necessary illusion or a systematic distortion rooted in the very operations of a social, political, or economic system (Dowling 1984; Larrain 1983 and 1996; Norris 1991).

The third Althusserian conception of ideology is more functionalist, viewing ideology as the means by which social relations are reproduced and maintained, as a mechanism of domination. Class society persists, people are kept in line and support the status quo, both through force and through ideology. The repressive state apparatuses (e.g., government, administration, police, courts, and prisons) provide the former, whereas the ideological state apparatuses or ISAs (e.g., religion, education, the family, communications, culture, and politics) yield the latter. From this perspective, ideology creates, "recruits," or "transforms" individuals into subjects "by that very precise operation which I [Althusser] have called *interpellation* or hailing, and which can be imagined along the lines of the most commonplace everyday police (or other) hailing: 'Hey, you there!'" (Althusser 1971, 174, original emphasis).

Individuals therefore necessarily live and work within the framework of ideology. They occupy their assigned places within the existing social order willingly, voluntarily, as if to do so were human nature, without giving their actions and beliefs a second thought (Callinicos 1976; James 1985; Therborn 1980). In this respect, then, Althusser's theory of interpellation conceives of ideology as a sort of confidence man—one who enlists your confidence in the game and reassures you that it is proceeding honestly and according to standard conventions, but all the while he makes sure that only he will gain in the end. Ideology thus gets us to consent to our own oppression, to engage in a process of willing subjection, to place imaginary flowers on our chains. Because every society must persist, "ideology (as a system of mass representations) is indispensable in any society if men [and women] are to be formed, transformed and equipped to respond to the demands of their conditions of existence" (Althusser 1969, 235).

Althusser's functionalism produces a fourth conception of ideology in his *Note on the ISAs*. In that work ideology is treated as the programmatic basis of a political party, as "the 'cement' (Gramsci) of a certain social group, which *unifies* it in its thinking and in its practices" (Gane 1983, 462, original emphasis). In this sense, then, proletarian ideology emerges as the ideology of the Communist party, an ideology with values different from those of bourgeois ideology. Proletarian ideology (like any other form of ideology) does indeed interpellate its subjects, but it does so in order to turn its subjects against the system, not to make them supporters of the system.

Althusser's own thought thus reproduced what Jorge Larrain (1983) asserted to be a characteristic development of Marxist ideology theory. According to Larrain, we have seen this tradition move from negative, critical conceptions of ideology, first articulated by Marx and Engels, to more neutral or even positive ones expressed by such thinkers as Lenin and Gramsci. Similarly, Martin Seliger (1976) has both traced and encouraged (within non-Marxist, social scientific theories of ideology) this sort of move from a restrictive (only some views, usually one's opponent's, are ideological) to an inclusive conception (all political views are ideological) of ideology. Perhaps because he was attracted to both, Althusser never did choose between a negative and a positive conception of ideology. Moreover, he never resolved the tensions among the four conceptions he did present, nor did he overcome some of the weaknesses of the Marxist tradition of ideology theory (Barrett 1991).

Ricoeur's discussions of ideology have followed a path similar to Althusser's. Initially, under the influence of Cold War politics, Ricoeur articulated a negative, restrictive conception of ideology—one that regards only certain kinds of belief systems as ideological per se, particularly those held by closed-minded extremists such as Nazis and Communists. For example, in a 1958 essay entitled "Ye Are the Salt of the Earth," Ricoeur observed that, in order to preserve itself, every ideology "has to falsify the truth, to falsify documents, to falsify history, as was done at the time of Stalin. It is a sort of refusal to face the truth" (1974b, 119). Since Ricoeur identified ideology with error, Bacon's idols, and Stalinism, he urged Christians (and others, presumably) to confront these falsehoods with the truth.

As his hermeneutic philosophy developed, though, Ricoeur acquired a more positive and inclusive conception of ideology. Focusing on such functions as social integration, legitimation, and distortion, he came to see ideology as a polymorphous phenomenon: First, ideologies represent a necessary symbolic and meaningful relation found among individuals in any social organization. Second, ideologies are dynamic, motive forces that impel as well as justify human action. Third, ideologies provide a simplifying schematic, a conceptual vocabulary or grid, through which individuals order, conceptualize, understand, and comment upon the world. Finally, ideologies represent the sedimentation of experience. Intolerant of marginality and resistant to change, they can impose closure or even blindness upon the perspectives of their adherents (Ricoeur 1981, 225–27).

The conclusions Ricoeur reached with this conception of ideology were rather predictable. First, he could no longer suggest that only certain belief systems are ideological, since "every kind of discourse, every mode of thought, may be schematized, typified, sedimented in the form of an ideology" (Ricoeur 1978, 51). Second, ideology must be seen as an inescapable phenomenon of social life, as the primary means of ensuring social integration, both establishing and maintaining a social group's identity from one generation to another. Finally, ideologies serve as the means by which authority justifies its claims to obedience—legitimating the established order and thereby both distorting our perceptions of, and integrating us with, that order's social praxis. The beliefs, images, and representations that we label ideology are essential for constituting both individual and group identity; no society can either exist or persist without creating them.

In key ways, the works of Althusser and Ricoeur illustrate the complexity of what Stuart Hall calls "the problem of ideology." In trying to understand how certain ideas manage to grip people's minds, how they come to prevail in various social and cultural settings, we must attend to "the concepts and the languages of practical thought which stabilize a particular form of power and domination; or which reconcile and accommodate the mass of the people to their subordinate place in the social formation" (Hall 1996, 27). As one moves from a negative to a positive conception of ideology, though, perhaps the political theorist must indeed "escape from the fascination exercised by the problem of domination, in order to consider the broader phenomenon of social integration, of which domination is a dimension but not the unique and essential condition" (Ricoeur 1981, 223). But before that escape may be possible, we must seriously evaluate the claim that there may be a nonideological place, an Archimedean point, from which we may critique the claims and pretensions of ideology. The conclusions we draw from that study most likely will shape our understanding of how new variants of a dominant ideology or public philosophy emerge.

SCIENCE, HERMENEUTICS, AND IDEOLOGY CRITIQUE

In many ways Althusser's work reestablished the social and theoretical import of ideology. He rescued the concept from antiquated notions of distortion and false consciousness and laid the foundation for a more functionalist approach to understanding ideology. This brought his views closer to those of mainstream social science, wherein ideology had become "an important variable in explaining conflict, consensus and cohesion" and "the decisive variable in explaining mass mobilization and manipulation" (Sartori 1969, 409; cf. Rancière 1974; Thompson 1978). Althusser's functionalist approach, nonetheless, also resulted in a fundamental theoretical ambiguity as he tried to maintain both a positive (ideology is indispensable to society) and a negative (ideology is a false or distorted perspective) conception of it. By trying to have it both ways, Althusser put himself in a bind.

At first, he made the relatively safe assertion that no society is without ideology. Yet, if this is the only assertion made, the theory of ideology begins to lose its critical edge. Regaining that edge then requires making the claim that ideology is the opposite of science—it is mere opinion rather than knowledge, falsehood rather than truth:

> The pressure of bourgeois ideology is such, and bourgeois ideology is so exclusively the provider of raw ideological material (frames of thought, systems of reference), *that the working class cannot, by its own resources, radically liberate itself from bourgeois ideology.* . . . For 'spontaneous' working-class ideology to transform itself to the point of freeing itself from bourgeois ideology it must *receive, from without, the help of science;* it must transform itself under the influence of a new element, radically distinct from ideology: science. (Althusser 1990, 30–31, original emphasis)

Though both the Marxist and the social scientific traditions have made similar claims, Althusser's version tends to undercut his own position.

What distinguishes science from ideology is, of course, an epistemological break, the achievement of an external, more encompassing perspective—for Marx, that standpoint was a proletarian one (similar claims have been made recently for a feminist or woman-centered standpoint). So far, so good; especially since there can be no innocent readings, whether of texts, of nature, or of society. By focusing on an epistemological break as the demarcation criterion for science, though, Althusser tacitly admitted that all perspectives are partial or limited, that all will be superseded in history by other, more advanced perspectives. Given his inability to see that Marxism itself may be superseded as a scientific perspective, and this tacit admission that all perspectives may be limited, Althusser merely replicated the very Hegelianism he frequently repudiated in his works. Hegelian teleology was thus smuggled into Marxist science, because the only perspective regarded as correct was simply the one most recently developed. Althusser's thought thus contains an unresolved tension between a theory of ideology that stresses its character as a necessary illusion (as opposed to scientific truth) and a theory that views ideology as the site or manifestation of the class struggle (Callinicos 1976; Sholle 1988).

Clearly, Althusser's efforts at theorizing an ideology critique leave something to be desired. Ideology critique simply involves distinguishing the true (Marxist science and philosophy, historical and dialectical materialism) from the false (bourgeois ideology). For Althusser, then, critique must be external:

> It is necessary to be outside ideology, i.e. in scientific knowledge, to be able to say: I am in ideology (a quite exceptional case) or (the general case): I was in ideology. . . . Which amounts to saying that ideology *has no outside* (for itself), but at the same time *that it is nothing but outside* (for science and reality). (1971, 175, original emphasis)

Only science can bring people out of the grip of ideology, a science whose intervention comes (in Leninist fashion) from outside. Nevertheless, given the far-reaching capacity of authorities and traditions to shape our lives through the ISAs and interpellation, Althusser remains quite pessimistic about whatever possibilities of liberation a proletarian science might provide (Eagleton 1991; Gane 1983; Hoy 1985; Smith 1984; Thompson 1978).

In his encounter with Althusser's thought, Ricoeur (1978a) clearly expresses his doubts that any nonideological science or social theory could indeed exist. The social sciences are too embedded in the lifeworld, in the praxis of ordinary human beings, for them to approach human affairs from an external standpoint like that of the natural sciences. Even a critical social science is not a viable option, for the very concept of critique in this sense presumes an unattainable standpoint of total reflection or absolute knowledge. After all, hermeneutic philosophy definitively shows that we cannot escape our belonging to the world, to our social class, or to our cultural tradition (Gadamer 1989c).

Is it possible, then, for there to be a hermeneutic critique of ideology? This very question was central to the famous debate between Hans-Georg Gadamer and Jürgen Habermas. For Gadamer the hermeneutic situation can be seen most clearly in the face-to-face dialogue, wherein the participants presume an intention toward under-standing—what Gadamer calls "good will." Moreover, in an authentic dialogue, any misunderstandings are readily corrigible, for we observe each other's gestures, body language, and patterns of intonation. We can ask questions of each other and thereby work toward building a common language (Gadamer 1984). But when we confront a written text, the chasm between author and audience is a wide one, and written words "risk misuse and misunderstanding because they dispense with the obvious corrections resident within living conversation" (Gadamer 1989d, 34). It is just this kind of misunderstanding that philosophical hermeneutics intended to avoid.

For some theorists, Gadamer's presupposition of this "good will" is problematic because the very goal of understanding is to make the un-familiar familiar and the puzzling intelligible. In this way Gadamer's conception of the good will ultimately becomes a will to power, a "means of making one's own understanding prevail" (Simon 1989, 165; cf. Dallmayr 1989, 91). Gadamer meets this challenge largely by re-asserting his claim that any attempt at communication presumes a de-sire to be understood; otherwise, no one would speak or write. More-over, the art of nailing someone down to something he or she said is not properly regarded as hermeneutics, which must instead be seen as "the art of grasping what someone has really wanted to say" (Gadamer 1989a, 118). Even so, Gadamer overlooks the possibility that in under-standing what someone has really wanted to say, one may well be claim-ing to know the other person better than she knows herself or he knows himself—a claim that itself must be supported and defended, not sim-ply presumed.

Thus, hermeneutic understanding quickly leads to assertions of au-thority, especially the ultimate authority of tradition, the context set by the voices of the past. Despite its conservative implications, Gadamer insists that his position is that, although authority cannot be evaded, it is not unlimited. Even within its ambit, one can nonetheless see beyond it—provided, that is, one achieves "the right horizon [i.e., standpoint] of enquiry for the questions evoked by the encounter with tradition" (Gadamer 1989b, 269). Hence, there is indeed an opening for critique. The model of conversation shows that our prejudices and preconcep-tions are vulnerable to challenge, for the "mere presence of the other . . . helps us to break up our own bias and narrowness, even before he opens his mouth to make a reply" (Gadamer 1989d, 26).

Still, the problem of ideology emerges with the task of interpreting "pretexts"—expressions whose meaning is not exhausted by their author's intentions and hence can be unmasked to reveal a hidden or deeper meaning. All ideological texts or discourses fall into this category, since the information they offer is merely a cover for a particular hidden interest. Ideology critique therefore involves a symptomatic reading (what Ricoeur called "the hermeneutics of suspicion") in which this hidden interest is revealed.

Yet the unmasking of political interest performed by ideology critique has, in Gadamer's eyes, at least two pernicious consequences. First, the practitioners of ideology critique frequently adopt an ideological attitude of their own. For example, the Frankfurt School's effort to construct a critical, emancipatory social science merely voices antibourgeois social and political interests, while masking its own tendentiousness with the honorific title of *critique* (Gadamer 1989d, 39). Second, ideology critique sets itself up as a standpoint free of ideology and thereby becomes another means for an authoritarian, Jacobinist assault upon the social order (Mendelson 1979, 67, 70). As a result ideology critique can lead to pervasive and unwarranted challenges to authority, neglecting the fact that authority is functionally necessary for the preservation of society.

Habermas came to engage hermeneutic philosophy as part of his effort to revitalize critical theory by returning to its original emancipatory project. In exploring the contributions hermeneutics could make to critical theory, Habermas largely accepted Gadamer's assertion of an underlying drive toward understanding present in any communicative situation. Yet, though the goal of communication is consensus, it cannot be consensus for its own sake. Any consensus must be reached for good reasons; it must occur through the redemption of claims to truth, rightness, and sincerity. Despite its critical potential, hermeneutics nonetheless fostered "a dependence of our interpretations on 'tradition' and 'authority' which seriously underestimates the necessary range of critique and the power of 'self-reflection'" (Ottmann 1982, 93).

In the course of this "linguistic turn," Habermas still had to face the question of the ontological status of communication, namely, "whether communication signifies a matrix underlying social interaction, or else a relatively extrinsic mechanism of social coordination" (Dallmayr 1987, 85). Naturally, as a critical theorist, interested in exposing and overcoming the reign of ideology, he has tended to stress the coordinating function of communication. Ideology thus comes to be seen as the presence of systematically distorted communication, in which people are unaware of and cannot voice their own interests or intentions, even as they speak (Bohman 1990; Habermas 1973 and 1989).

Since ideology limits whatever potential may be found in our conversational practices or in democratic discourse, a critical social theory must avoid "reducing the meaning complexes objectified within social systems to the contents of cultural tradition" and must examine dominant traditions "with a view to the relations of power surreptitiously incorporated in the symbolic structures of speech and action" (Habermas 1973, 11–12). Nonetheless, Habermas seemingly does not build upon this insight and develop a full-fledged theory of ideology, nor does he present a catalog of the distortions of and restrictions on existing discourses (Bohman 1990, 102–3). Habermas offers us less a theory of the distortions engendered by ideology, and more a theory of emancipation from those distortions.

A critical social theory can reveal "the normative power built into the institutional system of a society only if it starts from the *model of the suppression of generalizable interests* and compares normative structures existing at a given time with the hypothetical state of a system of norms formed, *ceteris paribus,* discursively" (Habermas 1975, 113, original emphasis). The problem then becomes how to identify those suppressed interests and the mechanisms by which the suppression occurred. One of Habermas's suggestions is that theorists expose the gaps between an ideology's claims and reality; that is, they highlight its systematic misunderstandings of social and political life. Yet, his most frequent answer is that we institute processes of critical self-reflection that help us overcome the forces of distorted communication and that we move toward processes oriented toward understanding, dialogic relationships and rational discourse among self-aware participants. In light of this regulative idea, social relations would be emancipated from ideology only in the context of an "ideal speech situation" in which the force of the better argument prevails and "in which a true consensus would be possible" (Sholle 1988, 24; cf. Bubner 1982).

Action advancing this emancipatory interest must therefore take place on a variety of fronts—scientific, interpretive, and political. No effective theory and practice can overlook the simultaneous need for accurate statements and theorems about the structures and processes of social life, authentic insights into our social and economic condition, and prudent decisions in matters of political strategy and tactics. Thus faced with a choice between reaffirming a tradition and separating from it, Habermas's position ultimately amounts to a "hermeneutic mediation [that] has to reconcile traditions, power and authority with our idea of the principles we would choose in a situation free of repression" (Ottmann 1982, 97).

Out of his examination of the Gadamer-Habermas debate, Ricoeur tries to develop just such a mediation—a critical, depth hermeneutics. Ricoeur (1974b) initially observes that because Gadamer's hermeneutics places people within traditions (wherein history and prejudgment precede reflection), the very possibility of ideology critique becomes questionable. Moreover, since Habermas's emancipatory interest is itself situated in the plane of communicative action, a critical social science finds itself in the very plane where the hermeneutic sciences are located.

For Ricoeur, then, neither the hermeneutics of tradition nor the critique of ideology has any valid claim to universality. Each is only a regional perspective (the one focused on cultural heritage, the other on institutions and domination); neither can be effectively divorced from the other, and neither offers a standpoint of total self-reflection. All knowledge, no matter how objective it appears, is marked by our belonging to a social class, a culture, a historical tradition. Nevertheless, through distanciation we can achieve a relative autonomy or critical distance with regard to that class, culture, or history—just as we can achieve it in relation to a text. In short, "distanciation, dialectically opposed to belonging, is the condition of possibility of the critique of ideology, not outside or against hermeneutics, but within hermeneutics" (Ricoeur 1981, 244). No worthwhile hermeneutics can be noncritical, and critique itself is dependent upon interpretive understanding.

Given the reality of domination, though, is critique really possible? This question is paramount for all of the theorists discussed previously because they all have come to regard ideology as a cultural template, a schematic grid through which one can order, conceptualize, understand, and comment upon the world (Geertz 1964). An ideology thus is a means for ensuring social integration, for maintaining group identity from one generation to another, and for justifying authority's claims to legitimacy. Since the essential function of ideology is a mediating, symbolic one, no society can exist or persist without creating the beliefs, images, and symbolic representations that coalesce into ideology. Ideological reproduction is a never-ending, continuous process.

When it comes to gauging the possibility of escape from the pathologies of ideology—its distortions, its conservatism, its legitimation of domination—Ricoeur was clearly more hopeful than Althusser. After all, ideology's distortions are "only a small surface of the social imagination, in just the same way that hallucinations or illusions constitute only a part of our imaginative activity in general" (Ricoeur 1981, 8). Viewing ideology from within the context of a more comprehensive "theory of cultural imagination" would recognize not only that ideology is part of the symbolic structure of social life, but also that the constraining, schematizing character of ideology is inextricably bound with the open-ended and imaginative aspects of utopia.

From a utopian perspective, contemporary realities and routines can no longer be "taken for granted. The field of the possible is now opened beyond that of the actual, a field for alternative ways of living. . . . The fantasy of an alternative society and its topographical figuration 'nowhere' works as the most formidable contestation of what is" (Ricoeur 1976, 25). Whereas ideology serves the function of social integration, utopia furthers that of subversion; whereas ideology legitimates authority, utopia imagines an alternative approach to power (Ricoeur 1986, 192).

Whether through the enlarged horizon of utopia or through the relative autonomy of distanciation, the critique of ideology provided by hermeneutics is nonetheless likely to be partial and fragmentary. Our utopian visions will no doubt bear the stamp of the world we inhabit, as we argue for changes that are not only substantial and radical, but realistic as well. The autonomous perspective we gain from achieving a critical distance will necessarily be only relatively autonomous, for we cannot create ourselves de novo: we cannot escape our own traditions. As Ricoeur rather ruefully notes, "the critique of ideology is a task which we *must* always start, but which we cannot ever complete" (1978a, 59, original emphasis). It is precisely this paradox that presents political theorists and political activists alike with the problem of ideological change.

THE PROBLEM OF IDEOLOGICAL CHANGE

In the preceding sections we have explored the thought of some important exemplars of Marxist and non-Marxist understandings of ideology. Remarkably, for traditions ostensibly at odds with one another, the conclusions they reach are similar. Our approach to ideological texts and discourses must strive to be both interpretive and critical. Yet, as we seek an alternative to the established order, the limits of criticism become readily apparent.

The history of Western Marxism in the twentieth century has long been one of trying to explain why the revolution did not happen where it was expected to occur. The continuing fact of an ever-malleable capitalism has remained a slap in the face of Marxists. As a result we have seen many analyses focused either on describing the latest form taken by capitalism (e.g., monopoly capitalism, late capitalism, post-Fordist capitalism) or on explaining why capitalism has persisted. In such explanations ideology often serves as the linchpin of domination, thereby making the critique of ideology necessarily the critique of domination. As Marx once observed: "Criticism has plucked the imaginary flowers from the chains not so that man may bear chains without any imagination or comfort, but so that he may throw away the chains and pluck living flowers" (McLellan 1977, 64).

Theorizing ideological liberation is therefore vital to the Marxist project. In Althusser's case, though, he erected his own unique roadblocks to a theory of ideological liberation. The sharp distinction between ideology and science suggests either that ideology has a significant ability to deform or limit its subjects ("there is no outside") or that ideology is simply a natural social fact, a species of harmless error. Either way, it becomes difficult to see how opaque relations could quickly become transparent, how people interpellated by authority could develop into oppositional subjects liberated from the grips of ideology (Best and Connolly 1979; Hartsock 1991). The problem for Althusserianism, then, is the one posed by Gregory Elliott: "Where within the cohesive, self-reproducing whole is the principle of its subversion and transformation to be found?" (1987, 180).

One solution to the problem has been to deny its premise, to suggest that ideological domination will always be incomplete. No matter the extent to which ideologies fulfill their role of subjection and qualification, societal efforts at domination will always be unsatisfactory in some fundamental way. Indeed, any "critique of ideology presumes that no one is ever *wholly* mystified—that those subject to oppression experience *even now* hopes and desires which could only be realistically fulfilled by a transformation of their material conditions" (Eagleton 1991, xiv, original emphasis). In other words, there are contradictions within society that no ideology can obscure forever. Even Althusser came to acknowledge that the "struggle for the reproduction of the ruling ideology is a constantly incomplete struggle which has to be resumed constantly" (Gane 1983, 455–56). Perfection is simply impossible.

The inability of ideological domination to be completed is not simply a brief for human imperfectibility. It says something fundamental about the very process of the reproduction of social relations. As Peter Berger and Thomas Luckmann (1966) note, reproductive processes will fail to convince or bring along succeeding generations, if only because they will not have the same experiences as earlier ones. Stories told by their predecessors simply will not ring true enough for them to be believed. Michael Walzer's prescient study (1983a) of Soviet ideology similarly suggests that no society can be completely totalitarian: dissidents will emerge, foreign ideas will seep through the ideological dikes, and faith in the system will inevitably falter.

Just as there can be no perfect domination, perhaps we must also acknowledge that there can be no complete liberation from an ideological tradition. Even if we do not postulate some ultimate "liberation" from orthodoxy, the problem for political theorists remains much the same. Although changing our way of thinking is central to fundamental political change, existing ideology and modes of consciousness also function as barriers to change. Our tools and methods of thinking are tied to the established order; we can think only in ways consistent with it. Further, the prevailing ideology short-circuits any serious reexamination of society's basic principles and practices, so that "those who try to contend against it are in many respects helpless to escape it" (Dolbeare 1974, 98).

How so? One answer may be suggested by Robert Lane's often overlooked paradigm of ideological change: "For any society, an *existential base* creating *common experiences* interpreted through certain *cultural premises* by men with certain *personal qualities* in the light of certain *social conflicts* produces certain *political ideologies*" (1962, 415–16, original emphasis). In Lane's account, patterns of life are made meaningful for human experience, are cognized and understood, in light of certain cultural premises. Sifted through the mill of personal qualities and social conflicts, these cultural premises thus create ideologies that provide more or less realistic interpretations of our experiences. Though an ideology will normally remain in equilibrium, many sources (e.g., technological innovations, economic developments, the diffusion of new ideas, altered child-rearing practices, or social and political cleavages) could provide the spur for ideological change. Still, for any ideology to be jettisoned in favor of another, the new one must fit with previously held values, beliefs, and ideas. In other words, the new ideology must be "congruent" with those previously held views in order to avoid producing significant cognitive dissonance among, and to have any chance of being acceptable to, the members of society.

What Kenneth Dolbeare saw as a "culture trap" I see instead as a *dilemma of congruence.* Advocates of political change seek to replace one ideological perspective with another, but they can do so only if the new perspective remains somehow congruent with the old. Demands for change that do not reflect the underlying logic of the dominant ideology will most likely fail (Crenshaw 1988; Piven and Cloward 1977). Although transcendence may be possible in the abstract, the limitations imposed by congruence make it largely impossible in concrete settings. Reformers may sincerely and regularly call for a change in consciousness, for new ways of thinking to fit with the new social realities we face, yet they have little choice but to work with the ideological materials at hand.

Ricoeur has argued, nonetheless, that a utopia provides the necessary external standpoint for the effective critique of ideology—an alternative and perhaps more comprehensive vision of the social order. As we have seen, though, it is very likely that ideology cannot be undermined solely from the outside. In part, as standpoint theory implies, that is because there are many outsides, too many positions competing for priority and advantage in the battle with orthodoxy (Hall 1985; Norris 1991). But mainly, ideology's apparent immunity to effective critique may be traced to the fact that, to some extent, we are all inside it. The dilemma of congruence discussed earlier thus reinforces the conclusion that there can be no outside, no Archimedean point from which to undermine and replace a dominant ideological tradition.

Nevertheless, within his critical hermeneutics, Ricoeur saw utopia as the primary source of ideology critique. How so? The answer lies in the unique contribution utopia makes in the process of critique. What utopia provides is an opening up of the possible, a transcendental conception that points toward the future, toward the society yet to be. It says that something is lacking in the current social order and that whatever is missing is capable of being replaced by human action. The danger, of course, is that the utopian vision we advance is inherently unrealizable, excessively self-contained and alien, escapist.

To avoid the escapist pathology, perhaps we require an immanent, connected social criticism (Eagleton 1991; Smith 1984; Walzer 1987). Our utopia must somehow be linked to the existing order of which it serves as a criticism, if not as the negation. Indeed, because of our embeddedness in cultural and ideological traditions, they must "serve as a reservoir of slogans, symbols, and ideals which both anticipate a better society and resonate with large numbers of people" (Mendelson 1979, 72). How then is an externally critical, utopian vision possible? How can we construct a vision of something yet to be, of something that perhaps cannot be at all?

Part of the answer may be found in one theory about how we began to conceive imaginary creatures, such as the gryphon or the unicorn. That theory has it that our imagination works by analysis and synthesis, by breaking things into their elements and recombining those elements in new ways. In short, we can imagine a gryphon because we know the nature of its parts—the body and hind legs of a lion, the head and wings of an eagle. In a similar fashion, we can imagine a society of authentic equality for women because we know the arguments for and the consequences of equality for men. In this way, perhaps, utopian elements can be drawn out of an ideology and become part of the critique of that ideology.

Walzer's understanding of social criticism underscores this account of the political significance of utopia. According to his view, the practice of social criticism involves "the identification of public pronouncements and respectable opinion as hypocritical, the attack upon actual behavior and institutional arrangements, the search for core values (to which hypocrisy is always a clue), the demand for an everyday life in accordance with the core" (Walzer 1987, 87; cf. Huntington 1981). At this point, though, the external ground of critique evaporates, for the social critic focused on hypocrisy must accept the modes of consciousness, the bedrock values, of an orthodox ideological tradition.

Still, it is possible for an ideology to be turned against itself, primarily because of the contradictory nature of its discourse. Any discourse is a tool that can be employed either for legitimating and reproducing a social order (in the language of Mannheim and Ricoeur, ideology) or for undermining and replacing that order (utopia). Moreover, the formulas of ideological discourses embody the polysemy (the existence of multiple meanings) characteristic of discourses generally. This means that any effort at ideological programming will inevitably send mixed messages. As Mark Billig and his colleagues observe, although ideology may lead to unthinking obedience and mindless ritual conformity, "it can also provide the dilemmatic elements which enable deliberation to occur" (1988, 31). That is, mixed messages sent by ideological discourse provide the interstices for creative thought, for recombinations of thought that can turn ideologies against themselves. Thus, fundamental change in a public philosophy will likely emerge "not through the substitution of the unprecedented for the familiar, but in the transformation of the present and in the development of structures and meanings already prefigured in today's society and discourse" (Bowles and Gintis 1986, 185; cf. Gramsci 1971, 195).

In moving from a negative to a positive conception of ideology, and in simultaneously assessing the prospects for emancipation, social and political theorists have necessarily forsaken the certain virtue of an external critique for the more limited possibility of an immanent, connected one. In this context the question is no longer how we can be freed from the influences of a dominant ideology; rather, in light of the dilemma of congruence, we should instead ask how a public philosophy can be transformed. With that question in mind, let us now examine three exemplary processes of ideological change that have helped shape the contemporary features of a complex, if not protean, American liberalism—namely, cultural transformation, oppositional politics, and conceptual critique.

CULTURAL TRANSFORMATION 3

Not only is it difficult to divorce the practice of ideology critique from the process of its hermeneutic understanding, but it may be fool-hardy even to try to separate the two. Just as problematic, it seems to me, is Karl Marx's claim that "ideologies have no history." What can such a phrase possibly mean? The claim is particularly puzzling when one considers that the very ideology of most interest to Marx (political economy) clearly developed and transformed itself over time—after all, there were more than a few differences between the political economy of Adam Smith and that of Jeremy Bentham, just as there certainly have been between these thinkers and their successors.

In short, our intuitions suggest that ideologies do indeed have histories. They develop, grow, and change over the course of time. But how? In his examination of the practice of social criticism, Michael Walzer asserts that "new ideologies emerge from old ones by way of interpretation and revision" (1987, 43). No doubt, but can we get a clearer picture of the kinds of interpretations and revisions that are made? Can we discover a pattern of ideological change, much as others have identified patterns of change in scientific theories? These questions are the subject of the remainder of this book.

Answering such questions cannot occur in a vacuum, though. Since this sort of effort requires a context, I examine the phenomenon of change in one particular ideology (liberalism), for a relatively short

span of time (from about the 1930s to the present), and in a single political and cultural location (the United States). This chapter and those
to follow survey some important developments in the history of modern American liberalism. But what follows is less a chronological history of liberalism than a reconstruction of intellectual attempts at effecting ideological change. My focus is on three approaches to that
task—approaches that I have labeled cultural transformation, oppositional politics, and conceptual critique. Although these approaches are
analytically distinct, insofar as they emphasize one or another aspect of
ideological change, they have not been mutually exclusive in practice.
Indeed, it would not be unreasonable to suggest that efforts to change a
dominant ideology, a public philosophy, or a political discourse operate
more or less simultaneously in all three realms.

FROM CLASSICAL TO PROGRESSIVE LIBERALISM

The paradigmatic instance of ideological change, in which the philosophy underlying American politics and policy was substantially revised
or overthrown, occurred during the rise of progressive liberalism. (It
should be noted here that students of ideologies have given many distinct labels to the type of liberalism that emerged in this century—e.g.,
progressive liberalism, reform liberalism, twentieth-century liberalism,
welfare liberalism, and New Deal liberalism. For the most part, all of
these labels refer to much the same set of ideas, and because the distinc-
tions among them are not critical to my argument, I will use the terms
more or less interchangeably.) The story of the development of contemporary liberalism began in the early twentieth century, whose first two
decades saw the emergence of urbanization, business mergers, interna-
tionalism, and governmental activism. Modernity and a reformist middle class had arrived, and their arrival meant not only the end of laissez-
faire, classical liberalism, but also the emergence of a new liberalism
and a new political order (Plotke 1996; Sandel 1996).

In the 1920s political leaders such as Herbert Hoover spoke content-
edly about how a new day had come to America. They believed that social and economic success rested upon the conviction that government's
obligation was to support the same private forces that had built the
American way of life. In the eyes of such thinkers, the United States
had grown prosperous and great only because of its liberal traditions of
individualism, localism, liberty, private enterprise, and property rights.

Left alone, such forces would produce a general prosperity that would filter down to the entire population and would permit most social problems and conflicts to simply work themselves out.

Despite such convictions, the theoretical transition to a new liberalism had already begun during the administration of Theodore Roosevelt, who believed that the national government should become the driving force behind American public policy. Social thinkers and journalists such as Herbert Croly, Walter Weyl, and Walter Lippmann echoed this belief and sought to articulate a new public philosophy. Their Progressive philosophy, known as the New Nationalism, aimed at replacing a self-fulfilling, automatic approach to political life with an approach that favored both conscious political action emerging out of a sense of national purpose and the rationalization of economic life through the efficient use of planning and administration. For some commentators, the ultimate contribution of this political theory was its accommodation of the increasing concentration of economic power that characterized the early part of this century. Rather than push for the decentralization of economic and political power, many Progressives embraced the idea that a stronger central government alone could counteract the growing strength of big business.

Other commentators have noted that, in the realm of political practice, the transition to a new liberalism probably began with the national mobilization for World War I, which highlighted not only the benefits of cooperation between government and business, but also some of the efficiencies of central planning. As a result national purpose and economic planning, long-standing dreams of American radicals, seemed at last to be at hand as the war's institutional structures showed the way to a new society. Yet, ironically enough, the war also undermined the spirit of the Progressive movement. Once-eager radicals soon turned from economic and political change toward plans for moral reform; lacking a coherent program, they moved from creative thought to mere sniping at conservative policy proposals. Eventually, Progressivism began to shade into a consumerist version of liberalism (one that triumphed during the New Deal) that merely used the federal government to provide tangible economic and social benefits to specific groups (Leuchtenburg 1958; Sandel 1996).

But the apparent demise of Progressivism occurred only because American liberalism had split in two and remained so until New Deal liberalism became the new orthodoxy in our public philosophy. As one scholar has observed, most liberal politicians of the day (George Norris, Robert LaFollette, and Al Smith, for example) continued to seek piecemeal reforms in policy areas such as public works and social legislation. Certain intellectuals (including John Dewey, Thorstein Veblen, Charles A. Beard, and others) continued to believe, nonetheless, that the central task was to formulate a new political philosophy. That new philosophy constituted a progressive liberalism that emphasized an affirmative role for a government that supported the increased role of groups in American life and that sought to be responsive to the less fortunate members of society (Allswang 1978; Plotke 1996).

This revived progressivism, this new version of liberalism, at first presented itself not "as abstract forensic ideology, but as a program of practical amelioration administered in a pragmatic spirit of social experimentation. Its high priest, if it had one, was John Dewey" (Bluhm 1974, 77). Dewey's central role was to crystallize the ideas of those liberals searching for a new public philosophy. Arthur Schlesinger, Jr., has noted that Dewey's "writings made clear to insurgents across the board—whether in philosophy or history, economics or jurisprudence or politics—what they were doing and what they were seeking. He extracted from their controversies a common thesis and a common faith" (1957, 131).

Even so, the place occupied by Dewey in the transition to a new liberalism has been in some dispute. Some students of American history and politics have consigned him to a minor role in the ideological transformation begun during the Progressive era, preferring to focus on more influential and politically connected thinkers such as Croly and Lippmann. In such accounts Croly's 1909 book, *The Promise of American Life,* serves as the primary marker of the advent of reform liberalism in the United States (Forcey 1961; Lustig 1982; Pells 1973). It was among the first of many books to argue that social and economic changes in American life required a new political order rooted in a new ideology of efficiency, rational organization, and a mixed economy. Because of the corporate or organizational ethos expressed in the book, Croly has usually served as the exemplar of Progressivism for those wanting to emphasize the new liberalism's managerial thrust and conservative implications—that is, the advent of a "corporate liberalism."

Other scholars, though, have given Dewey a more prominent place in the pantheon of new liberals (Diggins 1984; Ryan 1995; Young 1996). Acknowledging Dewey's status as the preeminent American social and political philosopher of the early twentieth century, these students of liberalism find it difficult to see anyone else as its chief advocate and theoretical embodiment. Few other thinkers set out the case against classical, laissez-faire liberalism with such consistency and force, and even fewer so clearly articulated the notion of democracy as a way of life and not just a form of government. As a result political thinkers looking for an early reform liberal who shares their democratic and communitarian sympathies have (not surprisingly) found one in Dewey. (In seeking relevant predecessors for their contemporary views, scholars behave much like the advocates for ideological change that will be encountered from time to time in this book.)

Though the relative importance of the many key Progressive thinkers cannot be finally decided in this study, I believe there are enough reasons for focusing on Dewey's views here with respect to the rise of a new or (as he called it) "renascent" liberalism. First, Dewey was one political thinker whose ideas resonated not only through the Progressive era, but also through that of the New Deal. Though he was ultimately critical of the New Deal for not going far enough toward a democratic socialism, for not developing a comprehensive political vision, he nevertheless shared some of its spirit with regard to the role and purpose of government. Further, his criticism of the New Deal did not mean that Dewey opposed many of its aims; indeed, his political writings and activities supported and encouraged many of the social, political, and economic reforms adopted by the Roosevelt administration (Bordeau 1971; Bullert 1983). Even though he often urged that a more radical course be taken, Dewey's support for a democratic socialism largely "took the form of an effort to revitalize and reconstruct the Anglo-American liberal tradition" (Westbrook 1991, 430).

Second, Dewey certainly understood perceptively the crisis then facing Lockean liberalism. With the many social and political changes accompanying America's industrialization and urbanization, the standard proclamations of laissez-faire liberalism in the United States increasingly diverged from actual economic and political practices. For Dewey and other reformers, that contradiction between our lives and beliefs, our institutions and attitudes, amounted to a pervasive and problematic "cultural lag." Amid America's mounting political, intellectual, and moral problems, Dewey consistently and forthrightly articulated the need for the kind of ideological change that occurred in the first half of this century. As he put it, one of his most important philosophical and political goals was "to find out whether it is possible for a person to continue, honestly and intelligently, to be a liberal, and if the answer be in the affirmative, what kind of liberal faith should be asserted today" (Dewey 1963, 2). Of course, what eventually filled that bill for Dewey was the sort of "advanced liberalism" or "new liberalism" put forward in Britain by Thomas Hill Green and others—a liberalism focused on government's role in promoting equal opportunity and effective freedom (Ryan 1995, 88, 316).

Dewey was thoroughly convinced that the discourse of liberalism was in severe trouble. Many symptoms of this trouble—for instance, the embrace of planning by major corporations at the same time as they opposed governmental efforts at social planning—revealed a very significant disjunction between our material and spiritual lives. Dewey and other critics in the 1920s and 1930s saw the lingering effects of the nineteenth-century version of American liberalism as repeatedly posing, in one realm of life after another, the nagging problem of cultural lag (Kaufman-Osborn 1984; Pells 1973; Ryan 1995; Tilman 1984). If the key problem of American life was a set of outmoded ideas and attitudes, as Dewey and other like-minded writers believed it to be, the only means of bringing the country into the modern age was to change that consciousness.

Perhaps the most troublesome symptom of liberalism's crisis could be found in the severely weakened loyalties Americans had to traditional values and creeds (Frankel 1977). Even where they were wrong, the liberals of the past at least had "a theory of politics sufficiently definite and coherent to be easily translated into a program of policies to be pursued." Yet, modern liberalism often appeared to be "hardly more than a temper of mind, vaguely called forward-looking, but quite uncertain as to where to look and what to look forward to" (Dewey 1930, 60). In many ways, though he was certainly not the only thinker to do so, Dewey sought to provide a moral and political vision for a generation of individuals with neither stable ideological roots nor meaningful direction in their political lives.

Unfortunately, this rootlessness appeared just as the atomistic, entrepreneurial individual of classical liberalism needed to give way to a conception of the individual as "caught up into a vast complex of associations" (Dewey 1930, 82). Forces of production were no longer organized and utilized by individual entrepreneurs but by huge joint-stock companies and monopolistic trusts. Economic activities were increasingly organized by corporate and consolidated, large and complex entities. Vital for one kind of society, the liberalism of Locke and Smith found itself impotent in the face of major social and economic changes. Though effective when its task was to open the way for new productive forces and modes of social action, when it came to "organizing the new forces and the individuals whose modes of life [were] radically altered into a coherent social organization, possessed of intellectual and moral directive power, liberalism was well-nigh impotent" (Dewey 1963, 53). Old beliefs and habits of thought that suited the needs and circumstances of times gone by no longer applied; instead, they simply "cumber[ed] the political ground, obstructing progress, all the more so because they [had been] uttered and held . . . as final truths, dogmas." Dewey explained, "No wonder they call urgently for revision and displacement" (1954, 145–46).

Every aspect of social conditions and human relations had changed, except our ideas and our ideals. Resolving this situation required, initially, that people understand the economic, demographic, and technological forces shaping society and culture. Rejecting both mindless support for the status quo and the impulsiveness of revolutionism, and consistent with his stress on problem solving, Dewey urged Americans to bring their economic and political conflicts of interest out into the open for free discussion and for the operations of organized intelligence. Of course, if this were an unqualified assertion that political conflicts (once made objective) can be resolved easily, it would be highly problematic (Damico 1978). Yet, Dewey's actual claim was the more modest one that resolving an ideological crisis involves tracing beliefs to their origins, exploring their conclusions and consequences, considering their mutual compatibility, and conceiving new possibilities (Dewey 1960, 107). Thus, a wholly empirical inquiry into the forces of social and economic change would not be completely satisfactory—if only because the significant problems faced by society are moral, philosophical, and ideological, rather than empirical in nature.

Dewey's approach to the crisis of liberalism, then, was simply to call for its reform and revitalization through the transformation of American political culture. Discontented with the way our civilization had defaced its liberal values and principles, Dewey sought to explore and eventually reduce the widening gap between cultural ideals on the one hand and social and political realities on the other. For Dewey, American liberalism's wheat lay with its central values of "liberty, individuality, and the freedom of inquiry, discussion, and expression. The chaff lay in the adventitious connection between liberalism and the legitimation of capitalism" (Westbrook 1991, 431).

In arguments reminiscent of John Stuart Mill, Dewey asserted that the classical liberalism that dominated American culture had once provided a great service for humanity. Weighing in on the side of freedom and limited government, it had emancipated individuals from all manner of traditional authorities. The problem, though, was that this same liberalism promoted not the general liberation of individuals, but only the liberation of those with property and privilege—a fact especially evident now that social life had become more corporate and freedom now required creating positive conditions for self-development. With the promise of emancipation unfulfilled, the faults of classical liberalism—which rested in its conception of freedom (negative liberty) and its understanding of human nature (atomistic individualism)—were now fully revealed.

Its chief defect was defining freedom almost exclusively in laissez-faire terms. Useful in the eighteenth and nineteenth centuries, when individuals sought relief from certain legal and political restrictions on their economic activities, the doctrine of laissez-faire had in its twentieth-century versions "hardened into the dogma of the freedom of the industrial entrepreneur from any organized social control" (Dewey 1946, 124). Dewey believed that this dogmatization of liberalism was possible simply because liberalism was unable to account for historical relativity. This inability let political concepts whose meaning naturally evolves over time (such as liberty) appear in the guise of immutable truths, thereby obscuring whatever differences there may be among the several dimensions of freedom—political, economic, and cultural.

Not only were we to acknowledge that the key concepts of liberalism are more flexible than we imagined them to be, but we also had to note that the specific social and political threats to liberty had changed. In Dewey's eyes, the changing social and economic conditions naturally and logically meant that our conception of liberty had to be revised as well. For example, when millions of people lacked basic economic security, freedom could no longer signify only the liberty of the entrepreneur—for that sort of liberty depended upon a system of power rooted in material inequality. A new definition of freedom was mandated, one recognizing that "actual and concrete liberty of opportunity and action is dependent upon equalization of the political and economic conditions under which individuals are alone free *in fact,* not *in some abstract metaphysical way*" (Dewey 1946, 116, original emphasis; cf. Dewey 1993, 158–60).

Dewey similarly criticized American liberalism's prevailing conception of the individual. In his view, expressed in the essay "Philosophies of Freedom," another key fallacy of classical liberal thought was that it saw "individuals as endowed with an equipment of fixed and ready-made capacities" (Dewey 1960, 269). Dewey's more process-oriented philosophy, of course, would have nothing to do with such static conceptions. One's individuality, along with many other attributes of mind and conduct, were social products; the dual influences of socialization and subsequent experience made us who we are. The notion of an atomistic, isolated, "rugged" individual was simply anathema to most everything within the compass of Dewey's thought.

The conception of a ready-made individual found in classical liberalism (and its associated Social Darwinist strains in American thought) simply had to be replaced by a more accurate view that stressed equal opportunities for the cultural and intellectual development of the individual (Ryan 1995, 301–2). Moreover, the very attributes associated with the rugged or pioneer individual were positively dysfunctional in the twentieth century. On the one hand they could no longer yield genuine individuality in the context of an increasingly corporate and conformist society; and on the other hand they could not fashion the consensus and cooperation needed in order for organized intelligence to function for the good of all.

Solving the problems of modern society thus required developing new conceptions of liberty and individualism. It also involved helping the public find itself through establishing a democratic community and creating a politically free, developmental culture. Plainly, such an enterprise could not rest content with a vulgar pragmatism that produced social reforms in the absence of any comprehensive plan (Dewey 1939 and 1963; Bullert 1983; Damico 1978). Because social legislation and institutional reforms must be improvised to suit momentary political conditions, they were not likely to reduce the ideological and moral tensions created by cultural lag. Instead, philosophical or ideological problems required more philosophical or ideological solutions (Shusterman 1994). Hence, Dewey argued for an ideological reconstruction that would develop a new version of liberalism interested as much "in the positive construction of favorable institutions, legal, political and economic, as . . . in the work of removing abuses and overt oppressions" (Dewey 1946, 136).

What sort of institutions did Dewey envision? Robert Westbrook has characterized Dewey's version of the good society as "a diverse yet harmonious, growing yet unified whole, a fully participatory democracy in which the powers and capacities of the individuals that comprised it were harmonized by their cooperative activities into a community that permitted the full and free expression of individuality" (1991, 164). In this context, too, we would substantially revise our understanding of traditional concepts associated with liberal ideology. For instance, whereas liberty once meant the individual's independence from social ties, it would now denote the fulfillment of one's human potential. Whereas equality once referred to mechanical identity or simple equivalence, it would now signify equality of opportunity. And whereas fraternity either was lauded as a noble ideal or was ignored as a vague sentiment, it could now refer to the sharing of social goods in a participatory community. Once we developed a common, democratic life in both economics and politics, then a true public (acting deliberately through organized social intelligence) and a genuine community (marked by authentic fellow feeling) would emerge at last (Dewey 1954).

Thus, Dewey's "renascent liberalism" would restore vitality and fullness to community life. Though skeptical of creeds and ideologies, Dewey nevertheless understood that they provide individuals with some measure of security and meaning, a sense of rootedness in society, and that they shape the processes and outcomes of policymaking in a democratic society. In other words, consistent with his view of "the philosopher as cultural critic," Dewey recognized that successful ideological change requires "a transformation of cultural values," a transformation that would necessarily build upon the democratic traditions already found within American life (Ryan 1995, 106; Westbrook 1991, 250). Because these same democratic traditions continue to resonate within our political culture, there should be no surprise that today's liberals are urged to revive some of the understandings of liberty and community advanced by Dewey and other Progressives (Dionne 1996; Sandel 1996; Sullivan 1986).

NEOLIBERALISM

More recently, contemporary liberals have confronted an ideological crisis similar to the one that troubled Dewey. In the early 1980s, for example, a loose collection of journalists, politicians, and academics took up the banner of "neoliberalism." Conceived as an effort to rejuvenate liberalism by discarding its outmoded features and accenting a different set of values, neoliberal beliefs have been aptly summarized by the journalist Charles Peters:

> If neoconservatives are liberals who took a critical look at liberalism and decided to become conservatives, [neoliberals] are liberals who took the same look and decided to retain our goals but to abandon some of our prejudices. We still believe in liberty and justice and a fair chance for all, in mercy for the afflicted, and help for the down and out. But we no longer automatically favor unions and big government or oppose the military and big business. Indeed, in our search for solutions that work, we have come to distrust all automatic responses, liberal or conservative. (Peters and Keisling 1985, 189)

Though they subscribe to the goals of New Deal liberalism, neoliberals have argued that the means (particularly those associated with the Great Society) to those ends have to be adjusted to fit new social and economic realities. Neoliberals thus have tempered their pursuit of liberal values with a realistic skepticism of government suited to a more conservative era.

Appropriately, the neoliberals presented several indictments of contemporary liberalism. One such indictment was leveled against a political pluralism in which organized interest groups place increasing demands upon the government, without ever considering whether or not their demands are indeed in the public interest. The advent of a "politics of selfishness" has fostered the rise of single-issue interest groups; an adversarial approach to government, industry, and law; and a society in which the primary motivation is greed and special privilege is the norm. According to the neoliberals, if the country was to survive, it desperately needed a renewed awareness of the limits of governmental largesse and a revitalized sense of the public good (Hart 1983; Peters and Keisling 1985; Tsongas 1981).

Neoliberals have also asserted that modern liberalism failed to give the United States a coherent ideological guide for policymaking. Rather than providing a lasting example of the benefits of affirmative government, it gave us a case study in the evils of big government. We have lost our competitive position in the world economy because government actions robbed people of incentives to work creatively and effectively, and thereby the government hindered the functioning of our most vital economic sectors. Although excessive governmental activism remained the chief culprit in America's economic decline, blame belonged as well to short-sighted managers and to greedy but unproductive workers. But regardless of who was at fault, economic revitalization required finding a balance between, on the one hand, a pure welfare state that ensures justice but destroys incentives and, on the other, a pure free-enterprise system that offers incentives but lacks a commitment to social justice. Thus, neoliberalism saw itself as a "third way," an alternative to both the bureaucratic good intentions of New Deal or Great Society liberalism and the laissez-faire coldheartedness of Reaganite conservatism (Fraser 1993; Rothenberg 1984).

The chief indictment against contemporary liberalism, though, was that its policies (by trying to maintain public support and funding for government programs) simply undermined traditional American values. Traditional values such as patriotism and progress had been forsaken for more recent ones, such as selfishness and stagnation. Personal sacrifice and commitment to the common good had been jettisoned for narcissism and self-interest. For many neoliberals, the key to revitalizing liberalism in the face of conservative successes was to return to traditional liberal values such as community, prosperity, rationalism, and pragmatism (Schurmann 1983).

Community, for the neoliberals, first meant a compassionate, humane concern for others, especially for the disadvantaged. Despite their critique of liberal policies and programs, the neoliberals reasserted their opposition to economic exploitation, racism and sexism, and political repression. Compassion alone was not all that was meant, though, when neoliberals invoked the value of community. Community in their eyes also required that social relations be rooted in a strong sense of both personal responsibility and national purpose. Neoliberals thus sought to create a society in which people would be bound by a universal code of conduct and citizens would consider the common good before they acted in the economy or the polity.

This characteristically liberal idea of a society marked by justice, equal opportunity, and civility was only part of the neoliberal vision. In practice, both justice and opportunity have depended upon improved standards of living; hence, economic growth and prosperity quickly became one of the most important goals of neoliberalism—to be achieved only through a coherent "industrial policy." Although a consensus on its details never emerged, the broad outlines of neoliberal industrial policy were sketched by a number of authors (Dukakis and Kanter

1988; Hart 1983; Magaziner and Reich 1982; Rothenberg 1984; Tsongas 1981).

First, neoliberal authors stressed that the federal government's fiscal policies should indeed try to stimulate increased rates of savings and investment in the economy. In contrast to the advocates of supply-side approaches, though, neoliberals emphasized that the location and purposes of investment were as important as its sheer magnitude. Second, they argued for government programs to deal with the very real social dislocations accompanying worldwide economic changes. Job counseling and retraining, improved educational standards and practices, and a general policy of investing in "human capital"—these became the hallmarks of neoliberal thinking. Finally, neoliberals believed it was time for a distinctive approach to economic policy, one that did not rely upon traditional (Great Society) liberal biases in favor of command and control, government regulation, or interest group competition. Neoliberal writers and politicians instead emphasized, time and again, that any coherent industrial policy could not hope to be successful unless it involved substantial cooperation among business, labor, and government—cooperation directed toward the public good.

In many ways, neoliberal discussions of industrial policy offered prime examples of the rationalist approach to problem solving that they tended to favor. Many neoliberals often expressed the belief that although the country faced serious problems, all our difficulties could be overcome—if only we thought clearly about them in the light of "new realities." Preferring the dictates of reason to those of ideology, neoliberals were not shy about showing their distrust of, and their displeasure with, the automatic responses of liberals and conservatives to our political and economic problems. Ideologically reflexive reactions to public issues simply prevented us from fully appreciating the situations we faced and from understanding what the national interest required. Only by taking a fresh look at our difficulties, by examining them in the light of reason and common sense, could we hope to offer solutions that actually work.

Their preference for rationalistic thinking about policy problems gave many neoliberals a reputation both for inducing sleep in their audiences and for favoring a new form of technocratic rule. Neoliberals sought to mitigate this reputation by pursuing one more goal—recapturing what many saw as the New Deal's original spirit of pragmatic idealism, a creative combination of both commitment and experimentalism. As Paul Tsongas put it: "We live in an era when pragmatism is vital, when a commitment to whatever policy has the best chance of working is essential, regardless of ideology" (1981, 232). Their pragmatic character allowed neoliberal policy prescriptions (from tax reform to military reform, from industrial competitiveness to national service and child care) to fall well within the mainstream of both the Democratic and Republican parties. Yet, this same pragmatic character naturally made neoliberal ideas virtually indistinguishable from those belonging to any other ideological tendency.

At a 1983 conference on neoliberalism, Hendrik Hertzberg acknowledged that the political difficulties faced by modern American liberals were primarily due to their inability to articulate an ideology, their inability "to make the connections between moral impulses and political actions" (Peters and Keisling 1985, 85). Desperately seeking an ideology, charged with creating a revised and revitalized liberalism, the neoliberals were better suited to creating a mood than to fashioning a new public philosophy. Pragmatic to a fault, neoliberals studied the details of specific issues and policies rather than reexamining the basic concepts of political theory. Unlike Dewey, who had taken philosophical notice of vast social changes in his effort to reconstruct liberal thought, the neoliberals merely noted recent social and economic trends and then invoked new formulas to counter what they saw as old dogmas. Neoliberalism settled for a facile grasp of "new realities" instead of striving for a deeper understanding of human needs and cultural aspirations.

One early partisan of neoliberalism, Gary Hart, has recently tried to correct this defect. Following the example of Machiavelli's *The Prince,* his most recent book offers advice to a hypothetical "new leader." Among the bits of advice, Hart includes a reminder that one can be liberal without being profligate and conservative without being mean—a necessary reminder because, regardless of one's ideology, it is clear that our "core public structures" (education, health, employment and training, public assistance programs) have declined to the point where substantial reform is absolutely necessary. Our goals of fiscal responsibility and civic spirit will remain as elusive as ever, Hart suggests, if we do not soon address the ideological problems rooted in such "mind-forged manacles" as "factionalism, prejudice, materialism, and preoccupation with amusement." Only a significant change in American culture, sparked and managed by a new leader, will let us "substitute for these manacles values of community, tolerance, deferred gratification, and authentic love of country" (Hart 1996, 20).

Once again, faced with an ideological crisis stemming from major social and economic changes, political thinkers have responded by calling for a cultural transformation. But whereas Dewey worked to describe the values his renascent liberalism would promote and to redefine the central concepts of liberalism, Hart has left the substance of his "new ideal" in a very amorphous state. All that is said about this ideal is that, by advancing its cause, the new leader could eventually lay the groundwork for "new value systems, new ideologies, and ultimately new public policies and programs" (Hart 1996, 183).

TOWARD A RESURGENT LIBERALISM

Largely inattentive to the requisites of ideological change, neoliberalism has generally remained a woefully underdeveloped public philosophy. As a sort of visionless pragmatism, neoliberalism has long needed someone to supply it with a theoretical perspective. Although some neoliberals recognized that need a decade ago, few made any headway on the project. Nevertheless, in the context of his diagnoses of the ailing American economy, Robert Reich (academic, pundit, and until recently Secretary of Labor) may certainly have done so.

For Reich (1983) America's economic decline can be understood only against the backdrop of the circumstances that brought about its earlier economic rise. During the late nineteenth and early twentieth centuries, the United States was poised to perfect a system of high-volume, standardized machine production. With abundant material and energy resources, highly mobile capital and labor, and a huge market for goods and services, it had a recipe for economic prosperity. That recipe was further leavened by the advent of scientific management and industrial coordination (the close links between business and government fostered by Progressivism). Yet, by the 1970s the U.S. economy experienced serious difficulties. High-volume, standardized production no longer guaranteed national prosperity but, instead, produced troubled core industries, a slowed productivity, declining use of manufacturing capacity, declining rates of profit, higher unemployment, a reduced standard of living, and declining shares of world markets.

Such problems stemmed largely from serious management failures in such areas as investment, cost management, pricing, international strategies, and labor relations. In terms reminiscent of Thorstein Ve-blen's distinction between business (making money) and industry (making things), Reich observed that during recent decades "product entrepreneurs" (e.g., inventors, engineers, production managers, and small business owners) have been steadily replaced by "paper entrepre-neurs" (e.g., lawyers, financiers, and accountants) (1983, 140–66).

This disturbing trend has been ultimately responsible for many so-cial and economic problems. Paper entrepreneurialism has wasted tal-ent by shifting the best people from product to paper concerns and thereby has also added to the economy's burden of debt. It has harmed productivity by creating a business community more interested in short-term profits than in long-term investments. Moreover, by treat-ing the production of social wealth as a zero-sum game, it has led to a rampant individualism and a "politics of secession" in which the eco-nomically advantaged have divorced their money and themselves from the rest of society (Reich 1989 and 1992).

Reich's point is that advanced industrial economies can become more competitive if they shift production to areas relying upon high-level skills and engineering. The United States has been unable to make this shift because vested interests and established values have prevented the necessary restructuring of relations within and among business, la-bor, and government. In general, our view of the American economy was shaped by how it operated during its post–World War II heyday. This perspective is now greatly mistaken, for there is no such thing as a national economy any longer. All productive activities now take place in ever larger and ever more complex "global webs" of shared informa-tion, talents, and problem-solving techniques.

Once one recognizes that there is no such thing as the *American* economy, one sees that we need a new way of thinking about our eco-nomic condition. A techno-nationalist or zero-sum nationalist ap-proach would return to the combative trade policies of the past. Such a move might well boost productivity and competitiveness by returning to high-volume production, by increasing capital mobility and prof-itability, and by cutting labor costs; yet it would do so only temporar-ily. A more cosmopolitan approach might encourage a sense of respon-sibility both for our own and for others' economic situation, but it could just as easily result in a political and economic paralysis because of the enormity and complexity of the world's problems—poverty, hunger, disease, militarism, and genocide, for example.

How, then, to revitalize the American economy? At first, Reich argued that it needed more coordination, rationalization, and government intervention—an industrial policy (Magaziner and Reich 1982). Somewhat later, as that concept wilted under the light of criticism, he began to advocate a "techno-globalism" that highlighted the cumulative technological experience of both engineers and production workers (Reich 1989). His belief was that, in a global economy, the primary question was not Who owns the means of production? but, rather, Who has the ability to add value during production? Most recently, Reich (1992) has branded his strategy a "positive economic nationalism" that would encourage public investment in worker education and training (especially for displaced workers) and provide public subsidies for high-value-added enterprises, yet oppose protectionist trade barriers.

This strategy also requires developing more egalitarian corporate organizations (Reich 1987). American enterprises, devoted to making money for their investors, typically have reserved management positions for creative entrepreneurs and labor positions for disciplined drones. Efforts to imitate Japanese management styles, by and large, have not fundamentally restructured relationships within the organization. As a result the only hope for fundamental change, Reich has said, lies in reviving from our liberal tradition the "deep strain of civic republicanism, of local political organizations, economic cooperatives, religious groups, and community associations, that has been as concerned with the moral quality of civic life and the relationships on which it is based as with the protection of individual liberties." Were corporate leaders to embrace republican values of equality and participation, a new approach to corporate life and organization could emerge—a "collective entrepreneurship" that understands that today "economic success comes through the talent, energy, and commitment of a team" (Reich 1989, 81, 85; cf. Selznick 1992).

Reich thus approached the contemporary crisis of liberalism by first examining the economic challenges facing the United States near the end of the twentieth century. This is, of course, not the first time that difficult economic problems have been accompanied by equally troublesome political and cultural challenges; indeed, since the Great Depression, the extent of government intervention in the economy has made political legitimacy now largely contingent on successful economic performance (Habermas 1975; Plotke 1996). When that performance falters, the existing regime may find it difficult to maintain its hegemonic status. Thus, a call for economic adjustment and restructuring may simultaneously function as a call for political and cultural change.

Obstacles to change remain, of course. A major one, it seems, has been a simple denial of the need for change, the refusal by management and labor alike to adapt to the new realities of a global economy. Even were people ready to adapt, effective cooperation between business and government would be hamstrung by a diffusion of political power that (in light of the proliferation of organized interest groups, the decline of political parties, and the general fragmentation of culture) continues to make concerted action difficult. Nor should we forget that traditional doubts about the desirability of "planning" have only been strengthened by the fall of Communism—widely interpreted as the triumph of laissez-faire capitalism over the dead dogma of centralized decision making. Given such obstacles to economic and political change, it is not surprising that neither an industrial policy nor a positive economic nationalism has yet won acceptance.

Even when we do acknowledge the need for an activist government (no matter how kind or gentle), ideological obstacles frequently bar the way to progress. In Dewey's day the constraints of laissez-faire liberalism made it difficult (as they do in our own time) "to discriminate between desirable government interventions and undesirable ones," a fact that thereby leaves "much of the initiative to political coalitions bent on preserving the status quo" (Reich 1989, 153). Underlying this decisional paralysis has been a cultural penchant for posing such false choices as opposing social justice to economic growth, government regulation to the free market, or the community to the individual. The only way out of this vicious circle (in which the excesses of conservatism are exchanged for those of liberalism, and vice versa) is to promote not only economic and political reforms, but also cultural and ideological change. In Reich's view, reformers seeking a path between Great Society liberalism and Reaganite conservatism simply have been "wrong to focus entirely on programs and policies at a time when the real challenge . . . is to enunciate an ideology appropriate to an era haunted by fears of survival" (1989, 240).

In short, the American liberal tradition must be reconstructed if we are ever going to get outside the cycle of decadence and regeneration. Nonetheless, when it comes to revising our thinking about the economy, we are quite literally prisoners of our own memories. Like parents who forever see their children as they were in early adolescence, we have fixed on a picture of the economy that was suited only to the era of high-volume, standardized production and large, nationalistic American corporations. It is Reich's view that this sort of "vestigial thought" has prevented us from recognizing that our images no longer fit reality; we cannot see that our child has grown up.

Our conception of politics has been equally limited, for we have tended to regard it either as a means for distributing shares of national income or for securing individual rights and interests. Rather, we should begin to stress the educative and civilizing function of political action and suggest that "it is precisely through broadly political activities . . . that individuals discover the subtler dimensions of their own needs and learn about the needs of others" (Reich 1989, 219). Within such varied contexts as trade unions and chambers of commerce, civic groups and election campaigns, individuals would no longer function as isolated atoms pursuing selfish desires, but instead would act as responsible members of a community—as people capable of balancing personal wishes and collective needs. The special pleadings of particular groups would be adjusted to fit more inclusive interests, so long as a fair distribution of benefits and burdens is assured and so long as institutions exist for making bargaining explicit and consensus authoritative. Political progress thus depends on constructing a process of democratic planning and public deliberation about both problems and solutions (Reich 1988; cf. Anderson 1990; Fishkin 1986). In such a polity, discussion of public policy matters would be tainted neither by domination nor by information management, and even its supporting ideology would be subject to thoroughgoing rational criticism.

The thrust of Reich's views, then, has been that the United States needs a new public philosophy in order to adapt to contemporary economic and political realities. The prevailing public philosophy argues that people are self-interested, that the public good is the sum of individual preferences, that voluntary market transactions are preferable to government dictates, and that government intervention in the economy can be justified only when it remedies market inefficiencies. It suggests that the great virtue of our form of government lies "precisely in its pluralism and ethical relativism, its *lack* of any overarching public ideas about what is good for society" (Reich 1988, 10, original emphasis). Such a view consistently understates the role of government, as well as average citizens and knowledgeable elites, in making good public policy. Moreover, by regarding the public interest as merely the aggregation of individual interests, our current public philosophy sees civic life as a zero-sum game wherein special interests protect their respective turf and possessions—not as an open, democratic deliberation over ends and means.

Nevertheless, despite the need for a new public philosophy, Americans have generally not been very receptive to the demands of formal political theory. In the United States what usually passes for political theory consists largely of parables, stories that embody a public philosophy by metaphorically expressing the underlying premises of our public and private lives. The stories we have generally reduce to a variant of four recurrent "morality tales": (1) the Mob at the Gates, wherein the United States is an isolated beacon in a world of darkness; (2) the Triumphant Individual, wherein success comes to those with initiative, self-esteem, and an inclination to hard work; (3) the Benevolent Community, wherein Americans are generous, compassionate, and helpful; and (4) the Rot at the Top, wherein powerful elites are irresponsible, corrupt, or decadent (Reich 1987, 8–13).

These tales have, in various combinations, set the terms of political debate throughout American history. In recent decades the liberal parable has focused on "wise and generous parents who skillfully accommodate the conflicting demands of their children, help their poorer cousins, and seek reconciliation with wayward relations" (Reich 1989, 278). Effective during the 1930s and 1940s, this liberal tale stressed the importance of solidarity and compassion as the prerequisites for survival and prosperity. By the 1970s, though, the story became less compelling as the social costs of reform and interest group accommodation came due, and as liberalism became identified with such character traits as arrogance, permissiveness, altruism, and guilt.

As the liberal tale lost credibility, a conservative story gradually began to win acceptance; the newer parable has spoken "of doting parents and their spoiled children, of public irresponsibility and social excess. But the parable also tells of a world 'out there' grown more ruthless and sternly warns that as individuals and as a nation we are in danger of losing our way" (Reich 1989, 275). This conservative story of discipline and responsibility, of course, characterized the Reagan era and has been revived with more recent Republican electoral successes. Unfortunately, neither the liberal nor the conservative parable has offered any effective guidance in a changing world. Instead, we have been moving from excessive conciliation to unreasonable assertiveness and have been responding to one parable's failures by reflexively adopting those of the other.

What, then, would a more adequate parable look like? For Reich a new public philosophy would strategically meet the challenges of global changes in economy, society, and politics. Evoking "dynamism and diversity" and rejecting zero-sum conceptions of life, it would "suggest instead the possibility of an enhanced quality of life for all, contingent on mutual adaptation" (Reich 1989, 287–88). Most important, the new parable would alter the content of our culture's four morality tales. For example, it would find no mob at the gates, only future partners (with their own interests, deserving of respect) in endeavors for mutual gain. It would place the locus of triumph not among isolated individuals but among competent, experienced, egalitarian teams. Community benevolence would be seen not as charity but as responsible caretaking, and a system of comprehensive and inclusive social insurance would be offered out of solidarity rather than altruism. Leaders would embrace the values of responsibility and stewardship, not those of greed and arrogance (Reich 1987, 242–51).

Whatever the precise details of its narrative, this reconstructed and resurgent liberalism would constitute a new political culture for America. Its communitarian ideology would acknowledge that economic survival depends upon the collaborative use of productive experiences and skills. Its republican commitment to public deliberation and social justice would ensure that benefits and burdens would be allocated equitably. Thus, the economic and political crises of liberalism are to be solved not only by the right kind of enterprise or polity, but also by the right kind of culture or ideology.

Undoubtedly, though, Reich's ideas do not constitute a full-fledged political theory. Although his writings have shown a consistent emphasis on such values as participation and deliberation, inclusiveness and equal respect, interdependence and mutual gain, his "resurgent liberalism" still has a truncated character—less so than other neoliberals, but truncated nonetheless. However laudable, his effort to transcend ideological and cultural alternation seems to have amounted to little more than a vague optimism for a brighter future, and his new parable (which appears to be a truncated version of a thin theory) ultimately reminds one of the description once given of the American vision of utopia—a place where nice people are nice to each other (Lane 1962).

Though he has not yet written a complete version of a new cultural parable, Reich's work has raised questions for our current parables to answer, and it has set standards for our institutions and practices to meet. In this fashion his ideas have done the work to be done by any ideology. His writings have provided a conceptual vocabulary through which to understand the forces at work in modern economy and society. Throughout his writings, his diagnoses of our economic problems have pointed to the cultural and ideological rigidities that prevent societal adaptation to the forces of change. Finally, he has presented (albeit in rough outline) an alternative way of looking at the world—one that emphasizes deliberative cooperation in both economy and polity and focuses on the value of human problem-solving capacities, skills, and experiences.

Yet, Reich has repeatedly shifted the ground of his critique of American society. At one time our problems may be traced to short-sighted managers and bureaucrats; at another, the guilt must be borne by abstract cultural images holding our minds hostage. Frequently, his prolific writings have suggested that Reich is more interested in challenging orthodoxy than in understanding it or proffering a coherent alternative to it. Perhaps we should not expect too much from any effort at ideological reconstruction. To do any more than raise the right questions may well be formalistic and utopian and hence contrary to the pragmatic spirit. Perhaps it is doubtful whether more could ever be achieved. Indeed, given the limited perspicacity of prospective vision, it is not surprising that an outline of a new set of cultural parables would fall flat.

CULTURAL TRANSFORMATION AND IDEOLOGICAL CHANGE

Despite its several problems, Reich's work is important because (like that of Dewey) it is cognizant of the need to match social, economic, and political changes by ideological or cultural change if liberalism is to survive. The emphasis on cultural transformation found in both Dewey and Reich, in both Progressivism and neoliberalism, suggests that key aspects of the process of ideological change may be modeled on the theory of scientific change presented in Thomas Kuhn's *The Structure of Scientific Revolutions* (1970).

Kuhn's approach emphasized several aspects of scientific practice that either forestalled change or accelerated it. In the history of various fields of inquiry, Kuhn found that scientific work had been guided by general outlooks or worldviews, which he called "paradigms." Such paradigms consist of identified problems and exemplary solutions, conceptual frameworks and methodological assumptions. Any given paradigm thus provides both a community of scientists and its work with a sense of purpose and unity.

In contrast to the conventional view of scientists as open-minded seekers of truth, Kuhn discovered that attitudes of dogmatism and tenacity permitted scientists to hold onto a paradigm long enough to work through the puzzles it had set forth. Work within the context of a paradigm was a sort of craft work, the kind of work that Kuhn labeled "normal science." It soon becomes clear, though, in the course of events described by Kuhn, that not all scientific puzzles can be solved within a given paradigm, and so certain creative individuals (often outsiders to a particular tradition or body of work) begin to criticize the paradigm's assumptions, methods, and solutions to problems both from within and from without. When anomalies (unresolved puzzles or contrary findings) grow too numerous or too troublesome, and when a suitably compelling alternative appears, an existing paradigm is jettisoned in a Gestalt switch not unlike a religious conversion.

Reacting to Kuhn's ideas, it seemed that each discipline developed a corps of scholars who sought to identify existing or potential paradigms in its practices. In the social sciences, the enterprise largely took the form of locating paradigms that would confirm their scientific status. Sheldon Wolin, for example, sought to prove that grand political theories (not coincidentally, these theories were viewed by behavioralist political scientists as the very models of nonscience) constituted "master paradigms," which would result in periods of "extraordinary science" when the "operative paradigm" of a political society fell victim to its anomalies (1980, 174–86). For the most part, though, these operative ideals and policies are uniquely adapted to fit worldly contingencies. The standard situation is one of political and cultural equilibrium, in which a public philosophy's deviations from fundamental principles are routinely explained away. As Martin Seliger has observed, this is why ideological change usually "takes the form of issue-reassessment rather than systematic ideological reconstruction" (1976, 260).

Still, in the face of significant social and economic changes, misunderstood by cumbersome dogmas and unconvincing parables, ideological reconstruction becomes imperative. Note how Dewey's dissatisfaction with laissez-faire liberalism and his efforts to overcome its problematic aspects very much fit this perspective. With major social changes necessarily requiring (in his view) corresponding cultural changes, the inability of the old liberalism to adjust to the dynamics of a new world simply meant that it was time for a new liberalism. What Progressive theorists like Dewey seem to have done, then, is to set the mood for a Gestalt switch in our political culture; the activists of the New Deal took advantage of that mood and thereby ensured a long-lasting cultural conversion by institutionalizing it in both the process and the substance of public policy. The whole affair proceeded in a manner not unlike that sketched in David Plotke's account (1996, 59–69) of the rise and fall of a political order through successive phases of building, consolidation, maintenance, and (eventual) decay.

Regardless of how often the mood for change may be set by political and cultural critics, successful efforts at ideological reconstruction clearly are not all that frequent. Indeed, instances of wholesale change in any ideological tradition are rather rare—within American liberalism, for example, there has been only one such instance in the last century. In the case of many institutions and procedures, the only change of which we are aware occurs incrementally. We more often experience long periods of normal science or routine politics than we encounter the sorts of intellectual breakthroughs associated with paradigm shifts. Dramatic alterations of consciousness, whether in the natural sciences or in political culture, appear so infrequently that "revolution" probably is not an inappropriate word to describe them.

This recognition brings to mind Walzer's view that new ideologies emerge largely through mechanisms of interpretation and revision. Our look at the reconstructive efforts of both Dewey and Reich suggests that Walzer very likely has it right. Their efforts at ideological change were stimulated by the fact that social and economic developments were met by little more than a stilted recitation of outdated verities. For these thinkers, social and economic progress was not possible as long as pathologies such as "cultural lag" and "vestigial thought" were promoted or even tolerated. The only option available for progressive forces was to embrace and encourage significant cultural and ideological change.

Notably, in the face of the contemporary crisis of liberalism, other thinkers have similarly encouraged American liberalism to abandon its Lockean origins in favor of a more modern and adaptive form. Substantively, this has meant that we must drop our prevailing value system— one that stresses individualism, property rights, market competition,

and limited government—in order to pick up a new one that emphasizes communitarianism, the rights of membership, community needs,
and affirmative government. Of course, since our political culture cannot make this shift as easily as individuals might purchase new clothes
or a new automobile, ideological reformulations are likely to follow a
three-step process: (1) people must understand how and why the old
ideology has faltered, and they must free themselves from its grip;
(2) people must understand which parts of the new ideology are inevitable and which are susceptible to some degree of modification; and
finally, (3) people must examine the transformation's implications for
themselves as individuals, as well as for their institutions and communities (Lodge 1975, 162).

Transforming a political culture is thus a difficult undertaking; its associated creation of a new ideology or public philosophy is no less so.
When it came time to cast aside an outmoded liberalism, neither
Dewey nor Reich (nor anyone else, for that matter) could do so completely—at least, not without risking their own irrelevance. Not surprisingly, their respective quests for ideological change each became defined as an effort to merely update liberalism, revise it to fit new
realities of social and economic life. How? As we have seen, both progressive and neoliberal thinkers chose to call for a cultural transformation in which old dogmas and ideological reflexes are cast aside in favor
of new ideals and concepts.

Naturally, this approach will likely raise the further question of
where to find the new ideals and concepts? Just as obviously, given their
embeddedness within a tradition, a hermeneutic horizon, political and
cultural reformers such as Dewey and Reich have little choice but to
work with whatever ideological materials are at hand. The task of
changing American political culture could no more require its wholesale replacement by an alien culture than recasting American literature
could involve making Esperanto the official language. As a result, each
of the calls for cultural transformation that we have discussed has
sought to rejuvenate liberalism rather than replace it. The very nature
of this rejuvenation and renascence, though, would produce a different
sort of liberalism than we had previously known; American liberalism
throughout most of the twentieth century has indeed been other than
what it was during the nineteenth.

Few observers would doubt that American political culture changed
in the early part of this century. Progressive liberalism emerged as an al-

ternative to, and eventual replacement for, the classical liberalism that began in the seventeenth century and had been a central part of the American experience. Given the dilemma of congruence, those who favored progressive views had to argue for changing liberalism all the while they remained within the liberal horizon. For Dewey and Reich, ideological change—even when conceived as cultural transformation—was pursued not only through a resurrection of liberalism's own strains of social democracy and civic republicanism but also through the development of new understandings of its central values and concepts.

Nonetheless, if we are going to fully understand ideological change, we must pay attention not only to instances of successful change (as with the advent of progressive liberalism), but also to instances of almost no change at all (as with liberalism since). We need, that is, to explain "both why our ways of thinking in some fields remain effectively unchanged over long periods, and also why in other fields they sometimes change rapidly and drastically" (Toulmin 1972, 122).

OPPOSITIONAL POLITICS

4

The difficulties associated with authentic cultural transformation have tended to reinforce pessimism about the possibility of ideological and social change. All too often, forces associated with the established order and its public philosophy have seemed too powerful to overcome. In such circumstances advocates of change learn anew lessons of strategic calculation and satisficing behavior, historical reflection and philosophical patience. Nevertheless, one can usually find at least some thinkers and activists willing to turn their political lemons into lemonade; there perhaps will always be some people who try to make a virtue out of stasis.

The United States in the 1950s was marked by just such circumstances and people. Many historians and social scientists argued that, after the defeat of fascism, a broad and stable consensus on social and political values had at last arrived. If there were no ideological challengers to the prevailing public philosophy, so much the better—for such challengers brought in their wake the perils of radicalism and extremism. Thus, the 1950s were said to mark "the end of ideology" (Bell 1960). In that period divisive ideological controversies had subsided, and significant political issues had been either solved or transformed into merely technical questions. Far from representing the end of ideology, though, the decade was a prelude to an era rife with ideological conflict and social change. To a great extent, contemporary political debates in the

United States can be seen as a residue of the intense social, political, and ideological conflicts that arose during the 1960s (Dionne 1991).

Even so, today it remains fashionable in some circles to see ourselves as living in yet another era in which ideology no longer has a place. Francis Fukuyama's essay on the end of history (1989) was one of many to proclaim the total success of liberal capitalism and its vision of society. The fall of Communism in Eastern Europe and the disintegration of the Soviet Union—"the most important political event of the twentieth century"—certainly offered the tangible evidence necessary to persuade the most skeptical among us (Kristol 1995, 123, 300). Even prior to Communism's collapse, it was common to assert (as neoliberals did) that politics in the United States needed to get beyond the rigid confines of ideology, or to claim that we could no longer afford to think in terms of the false choices our political reflexes produced.

Nevertheless, a closer look at the oppositional politics of the New Left and the New Right will show that ideology can never really die insofar as it is necessary for raising fundamental questions about political and social life, for restructuring political theory and practice. In many ways, the oppositional politics that began in the 1960s and 1970s has produced not ideology's end, but rather its transformation and further development. Exploration of these strains of political thought may therefore tell us something about the phenomenon of ideological change.

IDEOLOGICAL PARALLELISM

As some observers have noted, ideological debates in the decades after World War II have shown a significant degree of parallelism between what are otherwise opposite poles of political thought (Gitlin 1996; Schweitzer and Elden 1971; Westin 1971; Williams 1987). Apparently antagonistic ideologies have so often shared a rhetorical style or a mode of explanation that it is common for them to become all but indistinguishable. Indeed, despite the fact that the umbrella labels of Left and Right are given to various and sundry groups, these contrasting ideological positions have nevertheless produced a common critique of the bureaucratization, alienation, and stratification that mark modern society.

For instance, ideologues on both ends of the political spectrum have attacked the bureaucratization of American society, though the attack may shift from its dehumanization of people to its fiscal burdens or from its emphasis on social control to its attitude of paternalism. Both left and right ideologies have called for ending alienation by creating an authentic community, yet the foundation of that community may range from individuality and participation to religiosity and true Americanism. Finally, both the New Left and the New Right articulated the view that American society is dominated by a well-entrenched elite, although the precise identity of that elite has often been in dispute.

This apparent parallelism between ideological poles has made it easy for many Americans to either claim to be, or to seek the status of being, beyond ideology. But it has also made more difficult the task of assessing the success or failure of social movements arrayed in opposition to the dominant ideology. Sometimes it seems that the threads of the political fabric have become so interwoven that it would be impossible to trace any single one from beginning to end. Nonetheless, the questions we have raised about ideological change probably cannot be answered unless we make some effort to disentangle a few of those threads.

THE NEW LEFT

We can begin by noting the New Left's contribution to a diagnosis of the social and political ills of modern America. Bureaucratization was an early issue for the New Left, particularly since bureaucratic organization was seen as a hallmark feature of the socialist and communist parties of the Old Left. Run by small cliques armed with the tenets of democratic centralism, these parties were generally unable to adapt to changing circumstances and eventually were deemed irrelevant by most Americans. To the New Left, the political parties and organizations of the Old Left not surprisingly reproduced the sort of unfreedom found in Soviet society.

Yet, because of the advent of a corporate and managerial ethos in the 1950s, the unfreedom spawned by bureaucratization began to infect more areas of American society. Sparked by the moral example of those active in civil rights struggles in the South, and matured by their own idealistic efforts to organize the urban poor in the North, young activists in groups such as the Students for a Democratic Society (SDS) eventually began to acknowledge the campuses as both their social location and their political base. Concentrated among college students, the New Left naturally extended its critique of bureaucracy from the parties of the Old Left to the universities they inhabited. Soon, American colleges and universities were no longer viewed as idyllic and serene academic environments; instead, they were knowledge factories marked not only by widespread bureaucratization but also by increasingly overreactive responses to even modest dissent (Teodori 1969; Unger 1974). Having become the research and recruitment arm of the military-industrial complex, the nation's universities became potent symbols of coercive authority no matter where it might be found.

The pervasive bureaucratization of life in the corporation and the university bred other personal and social ills. Among them was alienation, usually conceived as occurring in several interrelated forms: alienation from oneself would appear whenever people had lost any sense of meaning in their lives, had no clear answer to the question, Who am I? Alienation would also occur when people felt isolated from others, when family and community ties had been severed amid a never-ending competition for goods and status. Finally, people who had become mere appendages of machines in factory production or who had become cogs in large bureaucratic organizations were also alienated. Lacking opportunities for creative self-expression and having no real power over their life decisions, they were likely to be deeply dissatisfied with their work and their lives (Gitlin 1969; Sargent 1972).

Despite the confidence and satisfaction found in the prevailing self-images of American society, the New Left both expressed and embodied the pervasive dissatisfaction with life it diagnosed as the condition of the average person. Rather than finding an energetic economy marked by affluence and plenty for all, it found substantial inequalities of wealth and income, desperate conditions of poverty in both rural and urban settings, and virulent racism in both the South and the North. Instead of a competitive yet beneficent capitalism, the New Left encountered an economy of monopolistic industries manipulating their potential customers through advertising and depriving their workers of personhood through the new management techniques of "human relations." Rather than working as a system of countervailing powers in which government balanced the interests of industry and the public, business was able to compromise the activities of its presumed regulators through lobbying and political corruption. And instead of a democratic society that gave everyone the opportunity to achieve the American dream, the New Left found a welfare-warfare state excessively concerned with social control both at home and abroad.

At the root of this inequality and domination was an ideology of "corporate liberalism" or "liberal corporatism." As Richard Flacks defined it, this ideology supported a political system in which the principal "policy issues are worked out at the federal level, formulated with the active participation of experts, and ratified . . . through a process of consultation among a national elite representing those interests and institutions which now recognize each other as legitimate" (1969, 192–93). In other words, the United States was ruled by an establishment (what the sociologist C. Wright Mills had called a power elite) that was primarily concerned with simultaneously preserving the profits of a corporate economy and meeting the needs of a military-industrial complex.

In a nutshell, the social and political activism we associate with the New Left, and the 1960s generally, fundamentally "developed as a response to numerous problems that had been festering in the nation for many years" (Anderson 1995, xxi). The specific manifestations of these problems were equally numerous; we can cite, for example, segregation and racism, the war in Vietnam and militarism, poverty amid affluence, and anti-Communist paranoia within the free world's largest security state. To remedy such a wide-ranging set of problems, the New Left's main prescription was a decentralized and participatory political system.

In the Port Huron Statement, for instance, the SDS advocated a society in which the individual would "share in those social decisions determining the quality and direction of his life," a society that would "be organized to encourage independence in men and provide the media for their common participation" (Students for a Democratic Society 1987, 333). The New Left ideal was not simply one of substituting local institutions for national or corporate ones, though; such a course would merely shift power from one set of elites to another without really changing society. Rather, participatory democracy involved developing mechanisms for authentic participation in political life and for popular control over collective decisions—the only way to transform in a fundamental way the power relationships prevailing in American society. As a time-honored cliché has it, the New Left believed that the cure for the ills of democracy was to have more democracy.

Though participatory democracy was clearly an important goal, it was not in itself (at least, not necessarily) the ultimate aim. Democracy was as often as not seen as a means to creating a genuine community of authentic, spontaneous individuals. But such a community (sometimes referred to as the "beloved community," following the usage of civil rights activists) could not come into being until people acknowledged their own alienation. For those sympathetic to the bohemian youth culture associated with the New Left, acknowledging and then escaping one's alienated condition first meant getting in touch with one's feelings, one's inner or true self. The available vehicles for such voyages of self-discovery were many—from rock and roll music to recreational drugs, from relaxing nature to intense association.

For many student activists, though, overcoming alienation required a more political course of provoking tensions between the rulers and the ruled, between the administrators and the administrated, in order to bring to light fundamental questions of power and control. Tactics such as shock, outrage, and ridicule were used in order to make people more conscious of conflict and alienation than they would otherwise have been. Once the initial hurdles of false consciousness and complacency were overcome, then, political action would serve as the means for creating both an authentic self and a genuine partnership with others. Ultimately, the New Left vision of community was akin to that of a close-knit group including everyone and sharing everything. Its establishment, it seemed, would end both competitiveness and alienation; community would both reconcile and merge the personal and the political.

The New Left ideology sketched above emerged partly because of changes in the economic and political character of the American middle class (Ladd 1978; Lejeune 1972). Whereas the middle class of the nineteenth century represented business interests and commercial values, the twentieth-century middle class began to have its roots in intellectual, educational, and social service pursuits. In an emergent postindustrial era, this new middle class not only directed economic and political systems, but it also appeared to advocate a new set of values—hostility to the status quo, reduced support for traditional bourgeois mores, and an acceptance of change in cultural norms and lifestyles. For some observers, the rise of the New Left thus marked the beginning of a pervasive, troublesome, and lasting "crisis of authority" (Steigerwald 1995, 243). For others, though, the youthful activists had simply revived a long-standing American tradition of "egalitarian irreverence"—a respect for the disrespect of authority (Gitlin 1995, 43).

The rise of the New Left has also been attributed to such social and cultural factors as a "demographic bulge, the delayed entry into the adult world, the encouragement of generational consciousness by advertisers, the cultural identification with outsiders and marginal groups, the inspirational example of the civil rights movement, and the paradoxical influence of cold war liberalism" (Isserman and Kazin 1989, 221). Unquestionably, these factors did much to produce a generation of activists who flocked to various causes and movements, as well as a generation of adherents who either accepted their leadership or seconded their voices.

Regardless of its economic or social roots, though, the contours of New Left ideology reflected the influence of two forces in particular. The first was an obvious yet annoying gap between American myth and American reality (Anderson 1995; Huntington 1981). The generation of young radicals that emerged in the 1960s was a generation that largely accepted the ideals promoted in civics textbooks, Fourth of July and inaugural speeches, and the works and teachings of countless historians and social scientists. That generation's spirit was well expressed by Carl Oglesby in a 1965 speech, in which he noted that, if anyone was to blame for an anti-American tone in his rhetoric, it was "those who mouthed my liberal values and broke my American heart" (1969, 184).

In this light it is indeed hard to imagine a generation more comprehensively and fully socialized into accepting the self-images produced by a social and political order. Interpellated as the heirs of a prosperity and an orthodoxy born of both sacrifice and providence, postwar youth were almost inevitably set up for radical disappointment once they encountered anew the gap between America's ideals and its institutions. If only liberalism had kept its promises, some have argued, it might well have forestalled the development of an insurgent political culture (Gitlin 1987, 135).

The second force shaping New Left ideology was what Paul Ricoeur has called "the utopian imagination." Like other modern utopias, that of the New Left was "directed against the abstraction, the anonymity, and the reification of the bureaucratic state" (1976, 26). Not that this antagonism was particularly unprecedented. Radicalism in the United States typically had defended civil liberties and individualism against the excesses of concentrated corporate or state power. Many philosophical and political predecessors could be found who, like the New Left, had linked alienation and bureaucracy, had been aware of the moral problems of affluence, and had advocated radical democracy (Steigerwald 1995, 121–27). Though not without precedent, utopianism was a significant feature of politics in the 1960s, if only because the very idea of utopia suggests the possibility of an alternative social order or another way of configuring power relations.

Of course, the utopian character of the New Left (at least, in its early phases) has never been in doubt. No one has suggested that its activists and adherents were down-to-earth realists or tough-minded pragmatists, for these were the very types (whether in government or business, in the military or the university) to which the New Left was opposed. Indeed, in its Port Huron Statement, the SDS lamented that the "decline of utopia and hope is in fact one of the defining features of social life today" (Students for a Democratic Society 1987, 331). To regard the New Left as solely an expression of the utopian imagination, though, consigns it to irrelevance as either an idealistic crusade (begun in innocence, ending in violence and pessimism) or a baby-boomer adventure (important only to its now-nostalgic participants).

If it is a mistake to write off the New Left's contributions to American society and politics, one must still address the question of just what those contributions have been. Maurice Isserman and Michael Kazin are among the many scholars who have done so, noting that despite many apparent political failures, "it is striking that while 'nothing' was accomplished by the New Left in its short life, everything was different afterward" (1989, 214). No explicit return to the status quo ante ever appeared throughout the reign of conservatism lasting from the presidency of Richard Nixon through that of Ronald Reagan. Instead, American politics and culture was substantially transformed in such areas as intellectual life, race and gender relations, foreign policy, and domestic politics.

The contributions of the 1960s to contemporary American politics and culture are many, indeed. Along with other social groupings, the New Left repeatedly called our attention to the sorry history and practice of discrimination and racism in the United States. Of course, given its origins and its alliances with the civil rights movement, this is not surprising. Moreover, the New Left's tendency to moralize about inequality, combined with the practical contradictions in its own organizations, eventually led to the rise of the women's movement. The unique perspectives developed by the latter have themselves changed American society, raising new issues and providing new insights in a variety of endeavors. Of course, it is just this sort of impact that more conservative thinkers and activists have decried.

In many ways, then, the whole tenor of our politics was forever altered by the sixties (Gitlin 1996). Since that decade contemporary life has seen opposition, negativity, and confrontation become the order of the day. A succession of public figures and social movements have used demonstrations and sit-ins, shock and outrage, in order to achieve their political goals. The moralistic and strident tone of today's debates not only over issues of public policy, but also over the actions and characters of political leaders, can be traced to the upheaval of the sixties and the cultural conflict that ensued. Unbridled individualism and extremism, a libertarian strain of thought, a love/hate relationship with government action, as well as a communitarian push toward unity and solidarity—all these can be found in the ideology and practice of the radicals associated with the New Left (and remarkably, but perhaps not surprisingly, the New Right).

In many respects, because there is so much variety to comprehend, evaluation of New Left politics frequently becomes little more than a matter of taste. Regardless of one's perspective, all a social and political commentator need do is to choose what aspects of the sixties to admire and what aspects to decry. Admirers no doubt remember the energy, the idealism, and the community of purpose found when moral fervor and political passion harmonized into committed activism for social change. Detractors, of course, highlight the "rebelliousness masquerading as radicalism," the culture of expressivism and exhibitionism that produced today's politics of identity and tribalism with its "narrow concern for fragmented and supposedly oppositional cultures" (Steigerwald 1995, 128; Tomasky 1996, 191).

Nevertheless, the ultimate contribution of the New Left may well be hard to gauge because its "influence on politics—and particularly on American liberalism—is so filled with irony and paradox" (Dionne 1991, 50). A prime example of this ironic legacy can be seen in the New Left's relation to the Democratic party and the mainstream tradition of progressive or New Deal liberalism. For many in the New Left, the Democratic party and mainstream liberals constituted the enemy, the primary threat to further progress toward peace and justice. Democrats were rendered suspect not only by their ties to the military-industrial complex, not only by their ideology of corporate liberalism, not only by their bureaucratic organization, but also by their repeated accommodation of southern conservatives. Without a fundamental realignment of the American party system, the New Left could not turn to the Democratic party as an authentic ally in the struggle to reform America.

Despite holding the Democrats at arm's length, the New Left ironically became identified with them in the popular mind, especially after

1968: "The riots, the welfare rights movement, the black power movement, student disorders, the sexual revolution, radical feminism, recreational use of drugs such as marijuana and LSD, pornographic magazines and movies, and higher taxes merged in varying degrees in the minds of many voters with liberalism and with the Left" (Edsall 1991, 72). Even with the breakup of the major New Left organizations, and perhaps because of it, both rightist and mainstream political observers came to lump together the political and cultural excesses of the New Left and Democratic party liberalism (not only the Great Society's social welfare programs, but also the moderate reform efforts of presidents Carter and Clinton). From this elision, it has not been too great a leap to identify the New Left with the Marxism and totalitarianism of the Old Left—Leninism, Stalinism, Maoism, and Castroism (Collier and Horowitz 1989).

Irony and paradox in the history of the New Left abound, then, not least because the movement appeared to betray its early, fundamental principles. One observation on this score is particularly apt: "The new left had begun by raising the 'feminine' values of cooperation, equality, community, and love, but as the war escalated, FBI harassment increased, and ghettos exploded, the new left turned more and more to a kind of macho stridency and militarist fantasy" (Evans 1979, 200). Another standard way of making the same point is that, whereas the New Left began in the spirit of community, idealism, and moral purity, it ended in a spirit of sectarianism, cynicism, and violence (Young 1996, 198–99). Though this betrayal of principles was no doubt accelerated by governmental intransigence, it may also be attributed to the rise of a new generation of leaders—a generation that television had schooled in the theatrical drama of political confrontation and the radical chic of suburban revolutionaries (Gitlin 1987).

In many respects, as Todd Gitlin has put it, the New Left initially appeared as "a movement of solidarity with the oppressed, though at times it searched for an ideology to transform itself into a movement for self-liberation" (1995, 98). Faced with the obvious difficulties of actualizing its dreams of participatory democracy (whether within its own organizations or within American society as a whole), it was perhaps only a matter of time until the path to self-liberation became more a cultural than a political one. The failure of the New Left can thus be traced most convincingly to the emergence of a split between political and cultural radicals—a gulf that left "the political radicals increasingly absorbed in their ideological pronouncements, the cultural radicals denouncing all politics as a snare and a delusion" (Lasch 1973, 340).

Unquestionably, this ironic and paradoxical legacy of the sixties and the New Left has helped make it difficult for us to clarify the status of the decade's social and political movements. But examining the New Left for signs of success or failure (defined in a narrow, scorekeeping sense) is, I believe, beside the point. Complex social and political phenomena typically result from a multiplicity of factors; they are rarely rooted in a single one. Moreover, for every positive contribution of the New Left, we can find a negative contribution. For every observer lauding the world-historical character of the movement, there is another lamenting its nihilism; for every praise intoned for the New Left's expressive idealism and commitment, there is a dirge sung for the loss of innocence its collapse represented.

Clearly, the reputation of the New Left is not an unalloyed one. What makes the New Left important for students of ideological change, though, is the very fact that its legacy is such a mixed bag. The split between cultural and political radicals that, according to Christopher Lasch, brought about its failure (it never ended poverty and injustice, never reached middle America, and never fully transformed political institutions) simultaneously made it possible for the New Left to succeed in some sense (it was able to develop a youth culture, change both music and mores, and transform higher education and intellectual life). This bifurcation in the movement (which later became two, three, many movements) may well be largely responsible for confining whatever contributions the sixties made to the superstructural level of ideas and culture.

A split or fragmented movement, though, offers a less persuasive explanation for the New Left's limited success in effecting ideological change. One factor that checked its ability to transform the liberal orthodoxy was the singular inability of its partisans to think deeply about practical issues of economics and politics. Indeed, it seems that among the remnants of the left even today, what passes for policy discussion is nothing more than the incantation of vague pieties or the recitation of endless and perhaps trivial critiques. Without any serious analysis of public problems and the policies necessary to solve them, radicals and liberals will naturally cede both the agenda and the dialogue to conservatives (Tomasky 1996, 113). The old saw of electoral politics—that you can't beat somebody with nobody—thus has considerable relevance for advocates of ideological change.

One other, and more important, factor that limited change can be traced to the ambivalent relationship the New Left had with liberalism. On the one hand it was partly from the liberal tradition of John Stuart Mill and John Dewey that the New Left derived its most basic values of political participation, civic republicanism, effective freedom, and individuality. Yet, on the other hand that very liberalism—in its more corporate or managerial guise—represented the status quo, the dominant public philosophy, the ideological and political enemy. Without the presence of a strong ideological counterweight, no doubt, any oppositional politics had little choice but to attack liberalism—whether it was conceived as the victorious consensus liberalism it was in the 1950s or as the guns-and-butter, Great Society liberalism it became in the 1960s. Nonetheless, it now seems all too clear that this incarnation of the dilemma of congruence certainly made the New Left's tragic efforts at ideological change all the more poignant.

NEOCONSERVATISM

As the New Left petered out with the modest success of the civil rights movement and the winding down of the war in Vietnam, a conservatism that had lain dormant began to be revived. Identifying just what constitutes American conservatism, dormant or otherwise, has usually been a difficult matter for students of political ideologies (Dunn and Woodard 1996; Harbour 1982; Van Dyke 1995; Young 1996). For some, during the period in which progressive liberalism was unquestionably regnant, any conservatism worthy of the name was simply not a viable option (Hartz 1995; Trilling 1957). The fact that the United States (unlike European nations) had not undergone a period of feudalism meant not only that socialism would always be viewed as an alien doctrine but also that conservatism had no native aristocratic class whose privileges and status it could defend. The kind of conservatism advanced by Edmund Burke and Joseph de Maistre, in reaction to the French Revolution, naturally had few advocates here in the United States. Even so, many traditionalist thinkers tried to find prominent figures in American political thought (notably, John Adams and John C. Calhoun) who embraced just this sort of conservatism (Kirk 1982).

Although many acknowledged the inappropriateness of European conservatism to the United States, the question of how to define or conceive a truly American conservatism remained. That question became especially pertinent during the 1950s and early 1960s with the rise of "radical right" tendencies (such as those associated with McCarthyism or, later, the John Birch Society) and with the forthrightly conservative presidential campaign of Barry Goldwater. Though conservatism was still often identified with lists of principles drawn from Burkean thought, with its aristocratic bias and organicism, scholars soon began to recognize that American conservatism was more attuned to the democratic character and individualism found in the political thought of classical liberalism. In his effort to comprehend the nature of conservative ideology, Samuel Huntington (1957) thus advanced a "situational definition" that regards conservatism as a style of argument that emerges whenever a status quo has been fundamentally challenged. Naturally, then, the specific tenets of conservatism would vary across time and place; whereas European conservatism defended the aristocracy, American conservatism would instead defend the bourgeoisie.

Certainly, American conservatives must face a number of problems as they try to preserve an essentially liberal order. Apart from the terminological confusion that besets anyone examining American ideologies, conservatives have found among themselves a persistent tension between the defenders of traditional society and the proponents of laissez-faire capitalism. A few decades ago, writers and thinkers associated with the *National Review* sought to overcome this tension by merging traditionalist and libertarian ideas into a conservative strain of thought they called "fusionism" (Brennan 1995; Diamond 1995). Adopting a united front in the face of their common enemy, communism, most of today's conservatives have long since accepted fusionism as just plain common sense. Indeed, whenever scholars try to define and describe American conservative thought, they usually do so in fusionist terms by focusing on interrelated political, economic, and religious traditions that emphasize common themes of constitutionalism, minimal government, and objective moral values (Dunn and Woodard 1996, 120–40).

Though fusionist ideas have become the conventional wisdom of American conservatism, tensions between libertarian and traditionalist camps still surface from time to time (Dionne 1991; Frum 1994). As a result our discussion of oppositional challenges to the orthodoxy of progressive liberalism must now focus on two related, but occasionally divergent, ideological movements. The first, a strain of thought that emerged among Cold War liberal intellectuals, has for some time been tagged with the label of neoconservatism. The second, appealing to rather different social groups, came to be called the New Right. Each in its own way arose in opposition not only to the problems of contemporary liberalism, but also to the ideological and practical legacies of the New Left and the 1960s.

The emergence of neoconservatism marked an important transition period in the history of contemporary liberalism. Upward mobility for the unionized segments of the working class, along with other social and economic changes associated with extensions of civil rights, had by the end of the sixties largely destroyed the unity of the New Deal coalition. Significant debacles in both foreign and domestic policy (e.g., Vietnam, social unrest, the War on Poverty) further undermined the appeal of liberalism in its Great Society variant. Further, as we discussed above, one of the central legacies of the sixties was a pervasive cultural crisis that many observers believed had significantly undermined the authority of traditional institutions (Habermas 1985).

In this context neoconservative thinkers began by offering, from the vantage point of disaffected liberals, a critique of the excesses of progressive liberalism—excesses generally associated with the social programs created by Lyndon Johnson's administration as part of its effort to construct the Great Society. Despite significant disagreements with one another, most of the neoconservatives "supported a minimal welfare state; all of them touted the superiority of capitalism and capitalist modernization; all of them vehemently condemned feminism, affirmative action, multiculturalism, and other adversary culture assaults on traditional Western values" (Dorrien 1993, 352). Associated with such publications as *Public Interest* and *Commentary,* the major figures of neoconservatism not only were upset with the self-destructive, bureaucratic course of liberal social policy, but they also believed that contemporary liberals had fallen prey to unpalatable cultural forces.

Since World War II the federal government had assumed significant responsibility for economic management, growth, and stability, as well as social welfare and social justice. Yet, by the 1970s, its efforts at economic management had produced an extended period of stagflation, while its egalitarian endeavors neither altered the distribution of income nor brought about an end to poverty and racism. In time, more and more Americans came to accuse this activist government of "reducing the quality of their personal lives through inefficiency, economic mismanagement of resources, excessive and inequitable taxation, unconstitutional invasions of privacy, and clumsy bureaucratic attempts to enact humane principles" (Clecak 1977, 74).

As liberals who had now been (in Irving Kristol's famous phrase) "mugged by reality," neoconservatives offered a hard-headed look at both the promises and the pitfalls of American public policy (Gerson 1996; Steinfels 1979). At first, in the 1960s, neoconservatives focused their attention on such prominent programs for the poor as public housing and Aid to Families with Dependent Children (AFDC, commonly called welfare), as well as such significant social issues as crime and urban unrest. There had, of course, been many long-standing criticisms of policy efforts in these and similar areas by social scientists and other observers of the American scene. Despite their liberal credentials and backgrounds, neoconservative thinkers began to take these criticisms seriously and to echo typical conservative themes about how government programs almost inevitably founder on unintended consequences and bureaucratic elitism (Friedman 1962; Hirschman 1991).

Although they were disturbed by many aspects of public policy, most neoconservatives retained a belief in some sort of welfare state (Kristol 1976; 1983; 1995). Their attacks on the programs produced by the War on Poverty did not at all affect their support for the more popular, social insurance programs associated with the New Deal. Government clearly had a role to play in helping those in need, but it had to learn to do so with minimal expense and bureaucratic regulation. Though subordinate to liberty, equality was still a prime goal of public policy—but it had to be conceived as equality of opportunity and not as the equality of result advanced by the many new claimants upon a government's resources.

Armed with recent academic analyses of advanced industrial societies, the neoconservatives accepted the view that these societies had become ungovernable because of an "excess" of democracy. Overburdened by an explosion in the number of interest groups, democratic governments in the West found it increasingly difficult to make decisions in the public interest or to assert common values in the face of conflicting demands. If not checked by a reassertion of authority, neoconservatives believed, a "revolution of rising entitlements" sparked by the very liberalism underlying the Great Society would soon make American society ungovernable (Bell 1978). One of liberalism's chief failures, then, was that it no longer acknowledged the limits of pluralist democracy. But neoconservatives did not reject democracy. True to their ideological roots, they could not deny the contribution made by liberalism in expanding the electorate and improving the standard of living of ordinary people. Though authority had to be reasserted (else order would collapse under the weight of popular demands), it had to remain democratic and popular if it was to grasp the true nature of the public interest.

Yet, it was not long before neoconservatives discovered a problem with contemporary liberalism more serious than an excess of popular democracy. Having successfully preserved both democracy and capitalism from the evil of fascism, liberalism was now failing to meet the threat posed by an "adversary culture" both in and out of government. This permissive culture born of affluence had produced a generation ungrateful for its advantages and therefore unmindful of the real dangers facing democracy and liberty in the world. In many respects, and perhaps without too much exaggeration, neoconservatism may thus be seen as the ideology of outraged parents responding to a revolt by their spoiled, self-satisfied children.

Permissiveness, of course, was not the only problem with this adversary culture. Troubling, too, was the fact that its bearers (rooted in the hedonism and nihilism of the New Left) had begun their "long march" through some of the key institutions of modern society—the academy, the mass media, and of course, the government. Convinced of their own moral rectitude, this emerging "New Class" of educated urban professionals was clearly at odds, if not at war, with the values of bourgeois society. As if that were not trouble enough, neoconservatives all too often found that the very liberals charged with defending traditional values had come to share and endorse the attitudes of the adversary culture.

Neoconservatism thus sought to call liberals back to their market-oriented and bourgeois roots. Government was not to be rejected out of hand, but it certainly could not be expected to solve all social problems. To expect it to do so would be to fall victim to contemporary liberalism's reflexive preference for elitist, bureaucratic, and national solutions to social problems. Indeed, government action more likely than not would make things worse through waste and inefficiency or excessive paternalism and dependency. What had to be rejected, unquestionably and authoritatively, was the adversary culture's flirtation with anticapitalist attitudes rooted in the socialist traditions of the European Left. Business was definitely not the root of all social evil; yet, their own socialist backgrounds and traditionalist sympathies would not let the neoconservatives wholeheartedly embrace business, either. At best, all they could offer was "two cheers for capitalism" (Kristol 1978).

Neoconservatism thus bears all the marks of a typically American

hybrid strain in political thought. Opposed to the expansive social programs of the Great Society, it wanted less to destroy the welfare state
than to make it more economical and humane. Desiring the level of
economic growth generated by the free market and entrepreneurial activity, it also believed that without a revival of traditional bourgeois and
spiritual values, capitalism would yield little but deepening self-cen-
teredness and nihilism among individuals and, as a result, a continuing
debasement of the culture.

Though akin to fusionism in its melding of libertarian and traditionalist themes, and more or less officially welcomed into the conservative
movement by the *National Review* in 1971, neoconservatism and its adherents have nonetheless been suspect among the defenders of what
some regard as an authentic conservatism (Gerson 1996, 43–46, 126,
309–15). These "paleoconservatives," associated with such entities as
the New Right journal *Chronicles* or the traditionalist Intercollegiate
Studies Institute, have long viewed neoconservatives as opportunistic
converts to the faith who are too tainted by liberalism to be trustworthy.

Whether or not the "neocons" are trustworthy, the "paleocons"
clearly touched upon a significant aspect of both the neoconservative
idea and the nature of ideological change. In what may be confirmation
of the charges leveled by the paleoconservatives, Kristol once suggested
that neoconservatism went beyond "contemporary liberalism in the
way that all reformations, religious or political, do—by a return to the
original sources of liberal vision and liberal energy so as to correct the
warped version of liberalism that is today's orthodoxy" (1983, 75).
Faced with a liberalism that no longer lived up to its self-proclaimed
ideals, there seemed to be little choice but to call it home again. Perhaps
because of their intellectual biographies, and perhaps because of their
hesitant reception by some conservatives, neoconservative thinkers generally have been ambivalent about whether their ideological mission
was to overthrow liberalism or to purify and revive it. One thing they
have been clear about is this: if to challenge the excesses of government
and an adversary culture means that one is no longer a "liberal," but a
"conservative" (with or without a prefix), so be it.

THE NEW RIGHT

Although neoconservatism gained a following among an impressive array of intellectuals, it generally did not capture the public's imagina-

tion. Nonetheless, as the neoconservative movement gained a voice in the Reagan administration, its unique ideological concerns were largely submerged in a general and more thoroughgoing assault upon liberal politics and culture. Marked by an unwritten compact between adherents of conservatism's social and economic strains and by a pragmatic alliance between conservatives in the Republican party and conservatives in certain religious denominations, the Reagan era brought the phrase *the New Right* into the American political lexicon.

In some ways a descendant of the fusionist conservatism of the 1950s and 1960s, the New Right also marked an important departure from it in both ideology and political strategy (Foley 1991; Himmelstein 1983; Lind 1995). One should note, though, that the New Right does not necessarily constitute a unitary point of view. Indeed, in one volume of essays on right-wing ideology, Roger Eatwell (1989, 7) has observed at least four strands of thought evident among the New Right in both European and American politics—libertarian (advocating the minimal state), laissez-faire (limiting state intervention in the economy), traditionalist (preserving institutions such as the family and religion), and mythical (eulogizing nation or race). Similarly, Noël O'Sullivan has found the right to consist of "three different and ultimately incompatible schools of thought"—the school of economic liberalism, the conservative school (including American "neoconservatives"), and the radical new right (1989, 170).

What could possibly unite these divergent strands of thought into an ideological whole? For most observers of American politics, unity among the various types of conservatives was rather easily achieved by a common enemy—the pervasive threat of Communism in the international arena and of socialism or collectivism in the domestic sphere (Brennan 1995; Diamond 1995; Gitlin 1995). Arthur Aughey has generalized this notion into the observation that the singular identity of the varieties of conservatism (both in Europe and in the United States) has been forged by its "engagement with opposing political principles, its intellectual and cultural contention with radical idealism" (1989, 103). Uniting the movement in the United States, then, has been a message focused on a litany of problems ranging from the growth of government to cultural and behavioral pathologies. In the eyes of many conservatives, the liberalism of the Great Society and the radicalism of the counterculture produced little but "perceived injustices, unrelieved exploitation by anonymous powers that be, a threatened future, and an insulted past" (Francis 1982, 66). Significantly, then, the New Right found itself developing cogent ideological critiques of bureaucratization, alienation, and class stratification just as the New Left had done.

Until recently, Americans tended to regard our comparatively modest welfare state as generally benevolent, albeit somewhat costly and inefficient. The prevailing notion was that, although government was vital to ensuring a decent life for people, it occasionally went too far. Conservatives of the Eisenhower era thus insisted that government operate under some measure of fiscal discipline and efficient, businesslike management. Clearly not prepared to mount a frontal assault on government amid the consensus and prosperity of the postwar era, some conservatives appeared to believe that the reforms and programs of the New Deal really had to be preserved—if only because most Americans had come to accept them as a routine part of life (Hamby 1992; Viereck 1963). Similarly, as we saw above, neoconservatives in the seventies also favored retaining the New Deal version of the welfare state, provided it could be managed more efficiently, although they certainly rejected its Great Society variant.

Rather than seeing government as bumbling but benevolent, though, the New Right that emerged most prominently in the 1980s came to see the welfare state as a threat to civilization itself—not only destroying the entrepreneurial initiative and basic productivity of individuals, but also undermining the traditional family by taking over its moral, educational, economic, and welfare functions (Eisenstein 1982, 77, 84–88). According to this view, government is "a Leviathan so gigantic and all-powerful as to engulf the nation, sapping the soul of the society, and existing for the benefit of a small clique of leaders of big government, big business, big labor, and, recently, big media" (Crawford 1980, 210). In short, what made the New Right different from previous variants of American conservatism was its populist character, its expression of the frustration and the resentment of "those sectors of society who feel a strong identity with the nation's history and ideals, but who believe that their society, and their place within it, is being subverted and corrupted from within" (Foley 1991, 140).

The New Right's oppositional critique of American society began with the sense that power had shifted from the leaders of local communities and their institutions (church and family) to distant government bureaucracies that "exist primarily to perpetuate themselves and to provide sustenance for those who belong to them, not to fulfill clear and limited goals related to the well-being of the community" (Wilson 1982, 117). Alien, if not opposed, to the spirit animating local communities, the unique set of values held by government officials reflects administrative interests rather than the needs of the people themselves. Thus, the modern welfare state "reduces citizens to clients, subordinates them to bureaucrats, and subjects them to rules that are anti-work, anti-family, anti-opportunity, and anti-property" (Gingrich 1994, 3). In short, government has become an intruder, a manipulative agent of unwanted social change, and a creator of dangerous social pathologies.

The New Right's disenchantment with government nonetheless represented only one symptom of broader feelings of alienation. Like its radical right ancestors, the New Right has largely been "a political revolt of the insecure and resentful," whose roots could be traced to "the incapacity of its adherents to come to terms with modern society—with the corporate state, with large business institutions, and with the organized labor movement" (Crawford 1980, 208). By now, the central theme of this revolt is familiar: time-honored values under relentless attack by elitist bureaucrats, intellectuals, and the mass media. The only lasting solution to the problem of such alienation is to recapture the bedrock values of hearth and home, the rugged individualism of the frontier, and the deeply felt religious faith that made America great. Of course, this reaffirmation of traditional values requires that a God-fearing, family-oriented, taxpaying middle class both challenge and overcome the well-entrenched New Class, which controls the life of the nation with its cult of expertise and its adversarial culture. Fortunately for New Right conservatives, the 1994 elections, in which Republicans gained control of both houses of Congress, were widely seen as one of many victories in the course of just this sort of challenge.

As the New Right tackled the familiar problems of bureaucracy, alienation, and class stratification, it followed a pattern of argument similar to that pursued by the New Left. To the extent that the New Right thought in terms of political structures, its preferred outcome has also been a form of decentralization. As Samuel Francis has argued, the New Right's fundamental aim must be "the localization, privatization, and decentralization of the managerial apparatus of power" (1982, 74). Bureaucracies should be dismantled, and devolution should be the watchword of a new political order. This rightist vision of decentralization invoked renewed support for local (as opposed to national) elites and institutions; not necessarily public control, mind you, but certainly decisions made by smaller units, where the prospect of public control was more likely.

Frequently, the central issue has been framed as a matter of either placing one's trust in distant government bureaucrats (who take your money and spend it on their projects) or placing that trust in the choices of ordinary people (letting you keep that money and spend it as you see fit). Calls for decentralization and the devolution of power thus become a brief for reviving an authentic community rooted in both individual responsibility and traditional values. Thus, the "cosmopolitan ethic" advanced by the adversarial culture of the New Class has to be replaced by a "domestic ethic" centered about "the family, the neighborhood and local community, the church, and the nation as the basic framework of values" (Francis 1982, 78).

The main source of this domestic ethic may be found in the collective experience of middle-income individuals with high school educations, employed in the clerical, sales, and skilled-labor sectors of the economy. According to Donald Warren, this segment of the middle class (populated by "Middle American Radicals") has shared not only a common socioeconomic status but also a common temperament: a feeling of "being caught between those whose wealth gives them access to power and those whose militant organization in the face of deprivation gains special treatment from the government" (1976, 14). This "middle-class squeeze" has been the subject of many magazine articles and recent election campaigns; it has also produced major differences in outlook between the upper-middle-class beneficiaries of the system and the lower-middle-class people who have paid the taxes and played by the rules. Whereas the upper middle class has tended to be hostile to the status quo, the lower middle class has largely supported it. Whereas the former has embraced social and cultural change, the latter has defended traditional value commitments and lifestyles. Finally, whereas the upper middle class has often supported the creation of new government programs to help people do what needs to be done, the lower middle class has increasingly expressed its cynicism about the ability of government to do anything right at all (Ladd 1978; Dionne 1996).

The tensions between these class elements, and between their respective viewpoints, have naturally led to repeated ideological skirmishes. These "culture wars" (as they have come to be known) have taken many forms—beginning with criticism of the New Left's deleterious effect on higher education (Bloom 1987; Jacoby 1994). The conflicts over cultural terrains have continued with more recent academic controversies over political correctness and multiculturalism, not to mention political debates about crime, welfare reform, school prayer, and family values. Throughout these debates, the New Right position has reiterated its common theme, returning to long-standing principles in American political culture. Notably, Representative Newt Gingrich, the Georgia Republican who became Speaker of the House, has made this theme central to his speeches and writings that focus on what he sees as the pillars of American freedom and progress—namely, "personal strength, quality, technological progress, entrepreneurial free enterprise, and the lessons of American history" (Gingrich 1994, 6).

The middle-class squeeze and its associated cultural conflicts clearly brought the New Right several political successes. Nevertheless, by the end of George Bush's presidency, the New Right began to be seen less as a monolith and more as a coalition of diverse interests. The fault lines of that coalition have since resulted in a number of minor earthquakes—activists associated with the Christian Coalition battled with economic conservatives for control over Republican party organizations in a number of states, prochoice Republicans urged that the stringent antiabortion plank in their party's platform be moderated, and explicit declarations of cultural war at the 1992 Republican national convention apparently precipitated an electoral debacle. Although its Reaganite roots have been rejuvenated by more recent electoral fortunes, the New Right continues to face significant problems.

Central to the practice of oppositional politics, the difficulties faced by the New Right can be reduced to two. One takes the form of a time-honored conflict between pragmatists and purists, between those who want to win and those who want to be right. Repeatedly, pragmatic conservative thinkers and activists have urged that the more alienated and alienating segments of the New Right (for example, Pat Buchanan's brigade of "peasants with pitchforks") set aside many of their preoccupations for the good of the Republican party. Though perhaps some movement conservatives have been unwilling to do so, a number of them have nonetheless moderated their rhetoric and supported more conventional policies and candidates in order to preserve their "seat at the table" (Reed 1996).

Still other commentators have stated that conservatives should replace their current short-term focus on winning elections (whether through supply-side optimism, Sunday school moralism, or a populist nationalism) with one "showing the public the necessary connection between the social pathologies it loathes and fears and the social programs it still rather likes" (Frum 1994, 201). Perhaps, as the purists believe, one should really prefer being right to being president. Yet, eager to submerge ideological differences for the sake of electoral success, and unwilling to abandon either of the paths laid out above, today's conservatives seem to believe that their standard bearers should try to become president by being right. If asked to choose between pragmatism and purity, or between resistance and reformism, they would simply opt for both.

The other key problem for the New Right is rooted in the multivocal character of conservatism itself. Absent any unifying force, the tensions among the three pillars of American conservatism (libertarianism, traditionalism, and anticommunist militarism) have reappeared and split the New Right into three not-easily-reconciled camps—optimists, moralists, and nationalists (Diamond 1995; Frum 1994). With fusionism seemingly falling on hard times, some erstwhile conservatives have begun to criticize their comrades. Michael Lind (1995), for example, has bemoaned the power of the Christian Right and the groupthink associated with a united front for electoral purposes. In his view, both of these forces have killed the only kind of conservatism he could still believe in—an "intellectual conservatism."

In contrast, other conservatives have tried to restore the movement's ideological vigor with a persistent devotion to a politics of ideas. Though a number of political thinkers and activists have tried to hold the pieces of conservatism together, Gingrich's self-proclaimed "conservative futurism" has certainly been one of the more noteworthy efforts ("New House Speaker" 1994, 3295). His ideological writings (Gingrich 1984 and 1995) generally relate a twofold tale—first, of how a venerable society has jettisoned its core values for pernicious ideas and questionable practices, and second, of how liberating individual and collective energies could transform the world and create a "conservative opportunity society." The keys to this transformation for Gingrich are many: spiritual renewal and the reassertion of American values; tax incentives to further savings and investment, property ownership, and entrepreneurial activity; and the steady promotion of a spirit of volunteerism and technological innovation.

In many respects, though, conservative futurism is a rather unstable compound. Like the New Left before him, Gingrich's effort to stay within the bounds of the American experience tends to push his conservatism "away from some of the more absolutist stances of the religious right and toward a far more libertarian vision" (Dionne 1996, 155). His preference for the libertarian ethos of Thomas Jefferson is quite at odds with his pleas for conformity to traditional values; his desire to foster a spiritual renewal conflicts with his embrace of secular revolutions in politics and technology. The dilemma of congruence we have previously noted essentially makes it difficult for any ideological movement to avoid the kind of internecine tensions now found among the New Right—tensions inherent in having to be simultaneously critical and congruent, oppositional and "system-supportive" (Diamond 1995, 6).

THE FAULTS OF THE OPPOSITION

The ideological and political stresses shared by the New Right and the New Left underscore the broadly drawn parallelism with which we began this chapter. In seeking to shatter the prevailing consensus of modern liberalism, each movement has unquestionably transformed the conduct of politics and the tenor of political discourse in the United States. Many more aspects of American life have been politicized—have been contested and made contestable—as a result of these movements. One consequence of their influence has been a polarization of political views and a hardening of ideological stances that has undermined the faith of many Americans not only in politics in general, but also in liberalism itself. Yet their efforts at creating new social institutions and practices, at overtly supplanting the old ideology through vigorous opposition, have been less than successful. Neither the New Left nor the New Right has sustained its momentum without setbacks; neither movement has been able to hold together its coalition of political and cultural radicals for very long.

Advocates of ideological change through oppositional politics thus face both theoretical and practical problems in moving from a normal politics that "addresses political experiences and problems within the framework of settled practices, institutions, assumptions, concepts, and values" to a more "revolutionary political discourse [that] involves the reinvention of conventional terms of appeal, contestation, and adjudication" (Dolan 1994, 15). Making that move, moreover, also means a direct encounter with the dilemma of congruence. For efforts at changing a public philosophy to be successful, the agents of change (the social groups whose ideas are advanced) need to hold views that are at least somewhat rooted within the dominant ideological tradition. Of course, they probably cannot do otherwise; for "even the most fanatical ideological movement, which seeks to remake completely the cultural capacities of its members, will inevitably draw on many tacit assumptions from the existing culture" (Swidler 1986, 278).

Agents of ideological change through oppositional politics quickly come to realize that it is difficult to escape the clutches of the very order they seek to overturn. One strong temptation is, of course, to give up the task altogether by adopting a political pessimism that underscores the durability of domination. Another calls upon change agents to embrace, if not celebrate, the fatalistic irrelevancy associated with aesthetic or cultural revolt. Avoiding these and similar temptations requires advocates of change to explore existing cultural ideals and shape them into believable, coherent narratives about a different kind of society. They need to discuss not the regulatory effects of power, but the processes and styles of empowerment; not the limiting effects of existing practices, but their liberatory potential—emphasize, that is, not the obstacles to ideological emancipation, but the *very possibility* of it.

In this light, one is reminded that utopianism was both the strength and the weakness of the New Left. For James Miller, the New Left at its peak "had some of the virtues of a utopian and romantic revolt—passion, moral intensity, a shared joy in the sheer process of change—but also some of its most glaring vices: intransigence, impatience, an irrational and ultimately self-destructive sense of self-righteousness" (1987, 326). In its dogged effort to "speak American" and to be "new," the New Left adopted the most utopian elements of the populist, egalitarian, civic republican, and revolutionary traditions found within American political culture.

By failing to link these elements with theoretical and practical insights, that is, by failing to be strategic, the New Left was unable to live up to its transformational promise. Indeed, given the ambivalent and ironic results of the sixties, a scholarly consensus has concluded that the New Left was most effective in the realm of culture, rather than the realm of political institutions (Anderson 1995; Birnbaum 1994; Isserman and Kazin 1989; Katsiaficas 1987; Steigerwald 1995). And despite claims that the activities of the New Left ended the war and exposed the hypocrisies of American racism, the broad movement it represented clearly foundered on its own contradictions. The New Left, with all the suddenness, energy, and longevity of an earthquake, both shook and split along its many fault lines—lines between the cultural and the political, the expressive and the instrumental, the personal and the political, making life and making history (Evans 1979; Flacks 1988; Lasch 1973; Morgan 1991).

In some ways, the New Right has also been more effective in culture than in politics. One can support this view by noting, say, the success of books such as Allan Bloom's *The Closing of the American Mind* and William Bennett's *The Book of Virtues,* or even the millions of listeners who follow the musings of Rush Limbaugh. Certainly, today's pervasive skepticism about the ability of government to solve problems in many policy areas has owed much to the influence of neoconservative and New Right thought (Gerson 1996, 349). Further, concern about crime, abortion, and other social issues has marked conservative politics since the days of Goldwater and Nixon. Yet, for all the talk of traditional or family values, the steady decline of American civilization has not been halted; if anything, it proceeded apace during the very time when the Right became politically ascendant.

Increasingly, the pressures of pragmatic politics strain the seams of the New Right coalition, as conservatives focused on economic issues do battle with those for whom politics is a moral crusade. Though the 1994 elections gave the Right a much-needed shot in the arm, its ideological weaknesses have to be acknowledged. Proclaimed commitments to consensual, traditional values are strikingly at odds with equally overt desires for political and cultural revolution. It is difficult to see how conservatives (whether neo- or paleo-) can reconcile images of a "gee-whiz," *Star Wars* kind of technological future with poignant nostalgia for the nineteenth-century America described by Alexis de Tocqueville (1969). As the neoconservatives recognized, the energies and forces of liberal capitalism frequently work to undermine not only the values of bourgeois society and what is sometimes called the Judeo-Christian ethic, but also the requisites of the republican tradition of civic virtue (Gerson 1996).

Nor can ideological change occur simply through straightforward and defiant opposition alone. Highly partisan debate and strident moralism tend to structure political discourse around a series of false choices, of alternating poles of opinion and policy. People then tend to become dissatisfied not only with the partisans themselves, but also with the ability of government to solve any problems at all and with the very notion of politics. Conservatism thus faces a choice between concerning "itself with specific abuses and not with grand visions" or committing itself to an appealing vision of an alternative future (Aughey 1989, 101; Woodson 1994). No matter how it may choose, the lingering danger for any oppositional ideology or movement is that it will become merely a partner in a well-choreographed dance and thereby serve as the resident critic of American liberalism.

Still, too narrow a focus on coalitional fault lines, too limited a view of the distinction between culture and politics, will overlook an important aspect of the legacy of oppositional politics. Movements such as the New Left or the New Right may well "define new epochs in the cultural, political, and economic dimensions of society. *Even in failure,* they present new ideas and values which become common sense as time passes" (Katsiaficas 1987, 8, original emphasis). Paradoxically, then, the very failures of these ideological movements may, in fact, be the source of their primary contributions to American political life and culture.

OPPOSITION AND IDEOLOGICAL CHANGE

Recent political history in the United States has thus demonstrated that oppositional politics, despite its possibilities, has some limitations as a mechanism of ideological change. Not only has each movement discussed above provided a stimulus for change, but our experience with each of them should tell us something about the process of change. That experience highlights, first, continued support for the Kuhnian accounts of ideological change discussed in the previous chapter, and second, an important qualification of those same accounts.

In chapter 3 the view of ideological change we drew from the advent of progressive liberalism fit nicely with Thomas Kuhn's musings about paradigm shifts in the history of the natural sciences. Central to that account was the notion that, like a scientific paradigm, a public philosophy hummed along quite nicely until it was progressively undermined by the cumulative effects of anomalies and then replaced by a new one in a political Gestalt switch. Indeed, this view represents one of the few consensus positions among contemporary social theorists today; it would be hard to find a theorist of any stripe who would disagree that "under certain conditions—massive demographic shift, war, sudden economic change—the old rules, cultural and social, no longer seem to apply" (Griswold 1994, 63). When these old rules no longer hold, when our expectations are not borne out by our experiences, in short, when significant anomalies have accumulated, people then try to create cultural, theoretical, and ideological innovations that would reorient their lives and practices. It was just this sort of consideration that yielded arguments for ideological change through cultural transformation in the thought of reform liberals like John Dewey and neoliberals like Robert Reich.

Among the explicit theories of ideological change that have been offered, Mongardini's (1980) account has similar Kuhnian overtones. Trying to explain a resurgence of classical, laissez-faire liberalism in the industrialized countries, he asserted that the meaning of an ideology can be traced to "the relations which are established with the other ideologies . . . and with the emerging groups" of a particular time and place. Thus, once a group gains political power, its ideology tends to alter its policy prescriptions and value assumptions in order to adjust to new circumstances. Over time, the group's ideology no longer is future-oriented and capable of adaptation, with the result that the political and social institutions under its control focus on maintaining the status quo, by force if necessary. Eventually, though, new needs emerge, new values are affirmed, new ideologies are advocated, and the cycle begins again (Mongardini 1980, 310–13).

Not only could this account explain the rise of New Deal liberalism, but it would not be hard to use it also to describe the emergence of New Left and New Right challenges liberalism. Just as the Progressive spirit of reform was shaped by the experience of an educated and moralistic middle class, so the New Deal embodied the coming of age of the American labor movement. For many observers, it was the very success of New Deal liberalism in opening doors to economic and social opportunity that undermined its position today, along these familiar lines (Dionne 1991; Edsall 1991; Tomasky 1996): the white working class benefited economically from the postwar boom and as a result moved to the suburbs and became bourgeois in habit and mind. Their baby-boomer children, bred in prosperity and imbued with the American myth, found both wanting and vocally and visibly rebelled in myriad ways. That rebellion itself was sparked by the obvious fact that African Americans did not share in many of the benefits of the postwar period, and when they sought access to some of those benefits, a seemingly inevitable backlash occurred. Amid increasing political and cultural demands by various groups, the left retreated into identity politics and the right began to wage an aggressive cultural war. The end result has been a strident and balkanized politics desperately requiring a new, more centrist and pragmatic way of thinking.

Another Kuhnian account of change can be found in the assessment of American politics offered by H. Mark Roelofs (1992), who has traced "the poverty of American politics" to its origins in both Protestant "myth" (ideals of popular sovereignty, community, equality, and justice) and bourgeois "ideology" (the pursuit of self-interest with maximum possible freedom). The result has been a myth/ideology cycle comprised of four stages. In the normal stage, tensions between the Protestant and the bourgeois traditions are seen as natural, legitimate, and somewhat remote. The tensions begin to heighten during an intensity stage, eventually reaching a crisis stage in which practical and theoretical contradictions are evident on a comprehensive scale. Finally, in the recovery stage, people put the tensions and contradictions behind them, and their polity returns to normal (Roelofs 1992, 57–59). Thus, Roelofs's view represents an equilibrium that follows the maxim, The more things change, the more they remain the same.

Though most accounts of ideological change in this vein result in equilibrium, Jack Goldstone (1991) offered a more dynamic understanding of the relationship between material and cultural forces in social and political change. According to his view, material factors such as demographic or economic changes are more likely to bring about state breakdown, whereas cultural factors are more likely to shape the eventual reconstruction of a state and society in crisis. This is not to say that ideology plays no role whatsoever in the various stages of state breakdown; it is to say, though, that the role of ideology differs across those stages. Sometimes ideological innovation responds to material forces, but at other times it is likely to follow its own dynamic patterns (Goldstone 1991, 457).

Looking back on our experience with the New Left and the New Right, we can see that Goldstone's perspective significantly qualifies the Kuhnian accounts of change addressed so far. After all, societies and economies undergo much more significant and more frequent transformations than does an ideology or public philosophy such as liberalism. Whatever material transformations do occur do not necessarily produce the ideological changes desired by political activists or expected by social scientists. Indeed, the very social and economic changes that have been credited with producing neoconservatism and the New Right have also been cited as factors contributing to the rise of neoliberalism, the New Left, and radical feminism.

Since change in advanced societies tends to occur when particular groups (adhering to this or that ideology) rise and fall in their access to power, the relative autonomy of ideology is frequently reaffirmed. Still, ideology can serve not only as an effect, but also as a potent cause, of social and political change. This is the point of Samuel Huntington's discussion (1981) of the gap between our political ideals and our political institutions ("the IvI gap")—the very sort of myth/reality gap we found evident in the rise of the New Left. Though established institutions in most societies will "lose their legitimacy because of a change in either the substance or the scope" of prevailing beliefs, the situation in the United States is that our institutions "confront an ever-present challenge to their legitimacy. The gap between the real and the ideal poses a distinctive national problem of cognitive dissonance" (Huntington 1981, 61–62). This dissonance is based upon the premise that our public philosophy is a unified, if not undifferentiated, "American Creed." When the IvI gap becomes too obvious or too intense to bear, political movements call us back to our basic values and possibly usher in an era of "creedal passion."

Though it acknowledges the relative autonomy of our political ideals, Huntington's view does not recognize another significant feature of ideologies—namely, the open texture and polysemy of discourse noted by Paul Ricoeur, among others. Open texture and polysemy, along with the dilemma of congruence, are features that may well suggest an alternative account of ideological change, which does not so much describe the dissolution and restoration of an equilibrium, the collapse of one paradigm and its replacement by another, as it speaks of the revitalization of ideological traditions that have been submerged (or even neglected) by a dominant orthodoxy. In this respect ideological critique must be both connected and oppositional.

Samuel Bowles and Herbert Gintis acknowledged the importance of this lesson when they observed that any given political discourse is, quite simply, a tool. It can be employed either to legitimate and reproduce a social order or to undermine and replace that order. In this context a new social order will usually emerge not through an extended period of upheaval and fundamental transformation, but through "the development of structures and meanings already prefigured in today's society and discourse" (1986, 185). In other words, oppositional politics will bring ideological change largely by reviving one or another currently submerged tradition located within the dominant public philosophy.

As several observers have noted, the New Left was certainly rooted in various strains of American liberalism (Ellis 1993; Jamison and Eyerman 1994; Miller 1987; Morgan 1991). Deweyan pragmatism and the independent and dissident radicalism of C. Wright Mills, as well as civic republicanism and populism, all had their influences upon the early New Left. In many respects the more advocates among the New Left sought to "speak American," the more deeply rooted in liberalism their ideology became. Hence, whether New Leftists discounted the likelihood of a conservative revival or welcomed it as something that would mobilize resistance, they were more dependent upon liberalism than they cared to admit. Although its democratic ideals permitted the New Left to address Americans in a shared idiom, liberalism's obvious political failures and social problems gave the New Left a foothold for a critical assault upon liberal institutions and practices.

Despite resting on such pillars of conservative thought as libertarianism, anticommunism, and traditionalism, the New Right has nevertheless also revived submerged traditions within American liberalism. Indeed, in the face of what many have seen as the collectivist strains in contemporary liberalism, the New Right has revived traditions that stress individualism and property rights, empowerment and populism. One key theme of New Right ideology has been its opposition to "big" institutions and distant authorities that populate the New Class of educators, pundits, media moguls, and bureaucrats. The New Right's majoritarian populism has been successful in making the Republican party a popular front composed of Christians and other cultural conservatives, libertarians and other economic conservatives, and its traditional allies in the business community (Wilentz 1995). This sort of populism has not always been majoritarian, though; it has also coexisted with a more hierarchical cultural strain marked by the acceptance of some aspects of the liberal orthodoxy. This hierarchical cultural element, then, has been "distinguished not only by its relatively uncritical embrace of competitive capitalism but also by its suspicion of governmental authority" (Ellis 1993, 118–19).

All in all, the experience of the New Left and the New Right has tended to support Michael Walzer's claims (1987 and 1988) about the practice of "connected criticism." In his view there are three tasks of criticism: "The critic exposes the false appearances of his own society; he gives expression to his people's deepest sense of how they ought to live; and he insists that there are other forms of falseness and other, equally legitimate, hopes and aspirations" (Walzer 1988, 232). Although this view sees the social critic as an individual (and a male one at that), social and ideological movements such as the New Left and the New Right might well be regarded as collective social critics.

For Walzer, the connected critic is one who remains a part of the community while criticizing his or her fellow citizens. This stress on the affective ties of the social critic to the community has come under scrutiny for precluding any chance of gaining a critical distance from one's own society and, indeed, for preventing the possibility of effective criticism. But even Walzer's detractors have had to acknowledge a version of the dilemma of congruence, namely, that social critics have to interpret and examine social practices in their participants' own idioms (Shapiro 1990, 290–96). Both of the ideological movements examined above have done nothing if they have not used the language of our prevailing cultural, religious, and political discourses.

Evans's study of the women's movement, nonetheless, implies that remaining within the prevailing idiom is not enough for creating an effective oppositional politics. Developing an "insurgent collective identity," she has said, requires the presence of several factors: (1) the social spaces necessary for developing a sense of worth, (2) role models showing how people can emerge from passivity, (3) an explanatory and justificatory ideology, (4) a communication or friendship network, and (5) a threat to one's new sense of self (Evans 1979, 219–20). Collective organization and action emerge when the possibilities opened by those social spaces, role models, networks, and ideologies are supplemented by social and cultural contradictions within the established order.

The practical import of the theory of connected criticism is to direct one's attention to the future, that is, to the possibility of social and ideological change. This focus on possibility recognizes that ideological change occurs not merely when people try to supplant an orthodoxy with an alternative point of view, "but also when they interrupt the ideological field and try to transform its meaning by changing or re-articulating its associations" (Hall 1985, 112). Given the dilemma of congruence, of course, the possibility of change depends upon the fact that ideological domination will always be incomplete, that there are contradictions within society that no orthodoxy can obscure forever. For example, to the extent that the social problems highlighted by the New Left and the New Right (i.e., bureaucratization, alienation, and class stratification) remain unresolved by the current political order, there will always be people who can and will adopt a critical or oppositional politics. The forces of opposition will most likely be aided by the mixed messages inevitably sent by ideological discourses, which provide the interstices for creative recombinations of thought that turn the discourses against themselves (Billig et al. 1988).

In the face of decades of political polarization, many observers of American politics have called for a return to a centrist, pragmatic, "non-ideological" politics that seeks common ground among disparate points of view. For some advocates of ideological change, such a public philosophy would mean that the critics of liberalism could only take up positions already located within the spectrum occupied by the dominant orthodoxy and thereby reinforce liberalism rather than replace it. The ultimate lesson of oppositional politics has to be that lasting political, social, and ideological change requires both critique and construction, both resistance and structural transformation (Nederveen Pieterse 1992, 13). The trick, of course, is to channel a utopian spirit in politically strategic directions without losing one's soul in the process. Perhaps a more philosophic attitude can provide the necessary hope, reason, and purity.

CONCEPTUAL CRITIQUE 5

In the preceding chapters two modes of arguing for, if not producing, ideological change have been explored. First, the writings of politically engaged, public intellectuals associated with Progressivism and neoliberalism have shown us that ideological change may appear as a species of cultural transformation. If the crisis of liberalism is not merely a political or policy crisis, but rather a moral one, then naturally change agents must seek to revitalize or transform (sometimes revitalize *and* transform) the dominant public philosophy. If yesterday's orthodoxy has become a fetter, if it has made it difficult to adjust to social, economic, and political changes, then we must adopt a discourse more suited to today's realities. But cultural transformation is a difficult process. Should one then despair about its possibility, a second approach to ideological change beckons. Since the political and social upheaval of the 1960s, oppositional movements such as the New Left and the New Right have focused their efforts on attacking the main tradition of liberal thought and practice. Direct opposition to a dominant orthodoxy, though, carries with it risks of alienation and irrelevance, on the one hand, or congruence and co-optation, on the other.

There is a third style of argument involved in effecting ideological change. This approach, employed by the dominant tradition's philosophical critics, uses the time-honored weapon of criticism to undermine the conceptual foundations of an ideology. This alternative approach seems viable, after all, not only because ideologies are largely configurations of concepts, but also because most work in political theory is premised upon unarticulated assumptions (Frazer and Lacey 1993; Freeden 1994). Sometimes those assumptions concern the nature of human subjectivity—for example, beliefs about whether human beings should be regarded as constitutively embodied and situated or as essentially disembodied and separated. At other times theoretical assumptions tend to be rooted in some of the key binary oppositions that mark the vicissitudes of Western thought—subject/object, individual/society, public/private, male/female. Finally, at still other times those same assumptions concern the relation of political theory to social and cultural phenomena, as with the many discourses and practices that inscribe women's oppression.

Most recent debates within the orbit of American liberalism, therefore, have focused on the legitimacy and validity of just such assumptions. Anne Phillips (1994, 74) has noted that, significantly, the arguments against liberalism have tended to focus on three elements: (1) its egotistic individualism that tends to deny community, (2) its neglect of social and economic inequalities, and (3) its preference for representative rather than direct forms of democratic politics. In many ways the recent history of liberal political theory has been shaped by sustained philosophical efforts to criticize some of its bedrock assumptions concerning the nature of the self, justice, and citizenship—particularly, the efforts made by two more of liberalism's ideological competitors, namely, communitarianism and feminism. In this chapter we explore the extent to which conceptual critique represents a path to ideological change.

COMMUNITARIANISM

More than two decades ago liberal political theory was resuscitated by the publication of John Rawls's *A Theory of Justice* (1971). Given his role in the revival of the enterprise of political theory, whether liberal or otherwise, Rawls's ideas virtually became identified with liberalism itself. Indeed, one contemporary theorist has used Rawls as his exemplar not only of Kantian liberalism, but also of several other, contradictory strains of liberalism—"libertarian," "egalitarian," and "minimalist" (Sandel 1996, 10–19). Although Rawls's conclusions regarding distributive justice were troublesome enough for commentators inclined toward a laissez-faire variant of liberalism, several theorists also found fault with the very assumptions Rawls made in order to arrive at principles of justice. Among those critical of the suppositions embedded within his contractarian account of justice, Michael Sandel (1982 and 1984), Alasdair MacIntyre (1984), and Michael Walzer (1983b) seemed to assert that the libertarian and the Rawlsian versions of liberalism (whatever their differences) both suffered from the defects of being overly individualistic and ahistorical. Stressing instead the importance of communal ties and obligations, those critics of liberalism in general and of Rawls in particular (however little else they had in common) collectively became known as communitarians.

What did the communitarian theorists want? In the words of one commentator, their goal has been to create a "politics that allows people to experience their life as bound up with the good of the communities which constitute their identity, as opposed to a liberal politics concerned primarily with securing the conditions for individuals to lead autonomous lives" (Bell 1993, 93). Whereas liberals have tended to view public life as a means to the achievement of individual ends or the protection of individual interests, communitarians have argued instead that social life locates one in "a web of affect-laden relations" (Etzioni 1996b, 5). In their view, the shared meanings and values, narratives and traditions, history and practices of a community fundamentally shape our very identity as human beings. The notion of community describes individuals in terms of "not just what they *have* as fellow citizens but also what they *are,* not a relationship they choose (as in a voluntary association) but an attachment they discover, not merely an attribute but a constituent of their identity" (Sandel 1982, 150, original emphasis).

Communitarian political thinkers thus believe that the life of the community is valuable for its own sake. Liberals, because of their more particularistic conception of the self, lack the conceptual tools necessary for comprehending public life in this fashion. As a result communitarians have spent much effort in attempting "to reconstruct important liberal ideas such as respect for persons, liberty, and justice on a more acceptable metaphysical basis, that is, based on a relational self and a non-foundationalist epistemology" (Moody 1994, 92). Rawls's version of liberalism, especially, has been faulted by communitarians for its reliance on a conception of an unencumbered, if not disembodied, self—that is, a view of the self as something divorced from the attachments and traditions that constitute it.

Communitarians, by and large, criticized Rawls's theory not because they felt that its conception of the self excluded feelings of altruism or even that it overlooked the possibility of individuals having community-oriented considerations. Rather, the problem was that both Rawls's assertion of the priority of right over the good, and his construction of the "original position" out of which agreement on principles of justice would come, appeared to assume the existence of an "antecedently individuated subject." Such a subject is one whose identity is not molded by its location in a community, but rather its ends and purposes are chosen only after its emergence as a distinct individual. Free and independent, this kind of subject is seen as having no aims and attachments it did not choose; such a self also demands nothing from others, save equal treatment and respect (Sandel 1982, 62, and 1996, 12).

Communitarian theorists have fundamentally disagreed with this Lockean view of the self. Taking their cues from a host of philosophers, social thinkers, and political theorists from Aristotle to John Dewey, communitarians have reasserted the self's socially constructed nature. The specific dimensions of our individuality are not ready-made, fixed, and eternal; rather, whatever unique qualities we have as subjects are due to environmental influences and the vagaries of experience. Recognizing that human beings are somewhat plastic creatures, shaped by the communities in which they are embedded, one communitarian thinker has suggested that "the nature of human nature" is "to be contingent and malleable, transformed as culture is transformed." Nonetheless, decidedly unlike Karl Marx, communitarians have not been willing to argue that there is no such thing as human nature. At the heart of their views can be found a somewhat functionalist conception: human beings try to fulfill a universal set of basic needs, and human nature has "a content that transcends cultural differences and provides material for moral ordering" (Selznick 1992, 134; cf. Etzioni 1996a, 164–67).

Insofar as a theory of justice was not rooted in this conception of the self, it clearly was flawed. Nonetheless, advancing a uniquely communitarian conception of justice proved to be more difficult than merely offering a sustained critique of the one proposed by Rawls. In general, the communitarian view of justice has been limited to the suggestion that our conception of it cannot be divorced from what we believe is necessary for human flourishing—beliefs that are, of course, inherent in the very narratives, traditions, and practices that constitute us. Individuation and communal bonds are inseparable aspects of human life, as noted above, and up to a point, one's individual rights and responsibilities to others tend to enhance one another. But because of the plurality of the communities in which one may live, and because shared understandings of the good life vary both across and within those communities, communitarians find it difficult to see how justice can be reduced to the terms of a hypothetical social contract. Though a communitarian theory of justice would probably endorse the notion of a "complex equality" that acknowledges that different principles must be applied in different spheres of life (Walzer 1983b), it rarely gets that specific. Instead, communitarians typically offer little more than a reaffirmation of the belief that a shared conception of the common good is a precondition for any community's possession of "rationally founded moral rules" (MacIntyre 1994, 8).

The communitarian idea of citizenship derives from this same ideal of the common good. Central to much of the renewed concern among scholars with the theory of citizenship have been the very issues, such as citizenship identity and civic virtue, that have been key to the communitarian critique of liberalism (Kymlicka and Norman 1994). In the course of this critique, for example, some communitarian thinkers have discussed such matters as what it means to be a member of a community and hence what relevance the concept of national identity may have in an increasingly pluralistic world (Taylor 1992; Walzer 1983b and 1989). Other communitarians have also tried to respond to challenges that their views amount to little more than a dangerous majoritarianism or an exclusive and coercive fundamentalism (Etzioni 1993 and 1996a; Sandel 1996).

Nonetheless, despite the centrality of communitarian thinking to much of the recent discussion of citizenship, articulating just what communitarians believe on this score is at times a difficult task. Certainly, like any democrat, they insist that the status of citizen is preferable to that of subject or slave. To be a citizen is to be actively engaged in the process of shaping the popular will on matters of public concern. Like egalitarian social democrats, some communitarians go on to offer a brief for both economic and political citizenship (Bellah et al. 1991, 107–9). In this light, citizenship requires just as much the possession of the effective liberty of an intelligent, self-directed producer or consumer as it does the cognitive and moral capacities of a responsible voter. And unlike more libertarian sorts of liberal thinkers, who stress values such as autonomy and consent, communitarians sometimes argue for the existence of obligations that are natural and intrinsic rather than voluntarily assumed.

Though there has been relatively little effort by communitarian thinkers to develop a coherent theory of citizenship, there has been some consensus among them on the relationship between notions of citizenship and the civic republican tradition (Barber 1984; Bellah et al. 1991; Sandel 1988 and 1996; Sullivan 1986). Here, communitarians are more or less agreed that citizens are made, not born: "More than a legal condition, citizenship requires certain habits and dispositions, a concern for the whole, an orientation toward the common good" (Sandel 1996, 117). Even though one's citizenship status may originate in filial ties and birthright membership in a community, or in the dictates of legal codes, it must nevertheless be continually nurtured through the various ties and attachments one has to particular people and practices. For communitarians, then, a vital public life is essential not only for genuine fellow feeling and human flourishing, but also for a self-governing, democratic politics.

Thus, the communitarian critique of liberalism's conceptual foundations has come full circle. Perturbed with liberalism's atomistic conception of the individual, communitarians have asserted the embedded character of a self situated within, and constituted by, a community and its stories. Such a self, then, is actualized only in the vibrant moral and public life of a formative community and its intermediary institutions. This rather Tocquevillean idea was for many readers the central message to be derived from the widely cited book *Habits of the Heart*. There, Robert Bellah and his colleagues (1985) criticized the rampant individualism of American culture and presented, through stories and interviews, images of the possibility of less isolated paths of life. The very sort of civic organizations and local communities that Alexis de Tocqueville (1969) had found so endearing about the United States in the nineteenth century were upheld once again as important models of vitality and activity, self-discipline and self-government.

This basic Tocquevillean vision has been reaffirmed in some key respects by other communitarian thinkers. Philip Selznick (1992), for instance, has presented a fairly detailed communitarian social theory, according to which moral selves can be nurtured and developed only in the context of moral institutions. In his view, once the practices of scientific management are replaced by more participatory styles of governance, and once organizations and individuals have become both responsive and responsible, we can probably overcome some of the essential tensions and difficulties of modern life. Only then can we safeguard human flourishing by creating a pluralistic, communal democracy. Similarly, Amitai Etzioni has sounded Tocquevillean themes in his portrait of an "authentic community" that balances autonomy and order, the needs of the individual and those of the community as a whole. The balance is achieved by a complex system of "layered loyalties," in which people simultaneously "see themselves as, and act as, members of more than one community" at any given time (1996b, 10).

Yet, for all this reaffirmation, the reliance of communitarians on de Tocqueville has not been total. For example, according to one critic of communitarianism, whereas Bellah and his colleagues previously harkened to de Tocqueville's celebration of the spontaneous activity of local communities, they have more recently shown a preference for the sort of national community found in the moral and political theory of Dewey (Frohnen 1996, 117–34). Not wanting to remain saddled with charges of endorsing either particularism or ethnocentrism, communitarians such as Etzioni and Sandel have embraced a more universalist vision of a pluralistic community of communities. Perhaps eventually encompassing all people, this ultimate community would have to be protected from tyranny by socializing people in traditions of mutual respect and civility, constitutionalism and civic participation, virtue and commitment to the common good.

The communitarians who thus make up "the party of the common good" (as opposed to the liberals who constitute "the party of rights") must necessarily tread a rather fine line as they try to revive America's dormant republican tradition (Sandel 1988, 116). The peculiar challenge for communitarians, then, is "somehow to conceive of community without appealing to examples of all-consuming public spirit such as ancient Greek citizenship or revolutionary republicanism with its Jacobin fervor, without idealizing primitive communities, and without resorting to organicism" (Rosenblum 1987, 153). Typically, the efforts of communitarians to meet this challenge have not produced very satisfying political thought. Neither Etzioni's invocation of the ideal of an "authentic community" nor Bellah and company's description of the "good society" go much beyond offering political platitudes. As a result, one is not surprised to find political thinkers arguing that communitarian theories of justice and the good, as well as conceptions of community itself, remain conspicuously "thin"—more illustrative and suggestive than illuminating and instructive (Cochran 1989).

Nevertheless, the communitarian critique has served as an important reminder that the liberal orthodoxy does not have an unassailable position. Communitarians have critically examined liberalism in ways that have revisited the metaphysics of atomistic individualism and the problems noticed previously by the likes of Dewey, T. H. Green, and John Stuart Mill. Communitarian appeals to the constitutive nature of tradition have replayed romantic, nostalgic themes similar to those sounded by Edmund Burke and other conservative theorists (Frazer and Lacey 1993; Wallach 1987). As a result, debates between communitarians and liberals frequently reduce to conflicts over whether the locus of sovereignty and control should remain with an autonomous individual or should rest with a superordinate community (Moody 1994; Reiman 1994). Though the liberal conception of individualism has certainly not been invariant over time, communitarian strains of thought have clearly provided a useful corrective to more atomistic conceptions of the self by reminding us that human beings are significantly and fundamentally rooted in the social world.

As often as communitarian critics have hit their mark, though, they have overstated or even misstated their case. Robert Thigpen and Lyle Downing (1987) have noted that communitarian critics sometimes have neglected the role individual autonomy plays in supporting mutual respect and empathy, as well as the function of Rawls's conception of an abstract self in guaranteeing the impartiality necessary to decision making in the original position. Also, Will Kymlicka (1989) has highlighted several inconsistencies within the theories advanced by communitarians—particularly the self-defeating admissions by Sandel and MacIntyre that individuals can indeed revise their socially given ends or question their culturally determined roles.

Yet another gloss on the liberal-communitarian debate suggests further that the whole matter has unfortunately been miscast. Taylor (1989), for example, has pointed to ways in which the debate has unconsciously merged positions on ontological questions (ranging from atomism to holism) with those on advocacy or moral issues (ranging from individualism to collectivism). The real issue, Taylor surmised, concerns the viability of a society steeped in the traditions of civic humanism and republicanism (which emphasize the interdependency of freedom and patriotism) relative to the viability of one rooted in procedural liberalism. The latter "conceives of society as made up of individuals with life plans, based on their conceptions of the good, but without a commonly held conception espoused by the society itself" (Taylor 1989, 172).

Michael Walzer (1990), too, has lamented that the debate has focused on ontological, rather than political, issues. Indeed, this focus has been self-defeating for communitarians, especially since an individual's ability to reflect on her or his own values does not support the primary role communitarian thinkers have ascribed to the self's socialization by the community. Moreover, the focus on ontology does not get us very far in those public matters of utmost concern—for the "central issue for political theory is not the constitution of the self but the connection of constituted selves, the pattern of social relations" (Walzer 1990, 21). As such, one might propose that communitarian theorists should begin to ponder the extent to which dissociation and separation actually characterize social life, as well as the extent to which these liberal ailments can, in fact, be remedied by a communitarian prescription.

From its beginnings in abstruse philosophical critique, communitarianism has recently developed an identity as something of a social movement "aimed at shoring up the moral, social, and political environment. Part change of heart, part renewal of social bonds, part reform of public life" was how Etzioni (1993, 247) described the nature of this effort. To further such goals, these "movement communitarians" have issued a manifesto or platform, produced a public affairs journal *(The Responsive Community),* and published numerous op-ed pieces on a host of issues. Emphasizing the ethics of responsibility rather than the rhetoric of individual rights, movement communitarians have called for an extensive program of political and social change.

Characteristically, their proposals for change have sought a middle ground between the polarized (and occasionally "false") choices offered in most contemporary debates. For example, communitarians would allow a moment of silence rather than a prescribed prayer in public schools—thereby acknowledging the importance of teaching moral values without giving anything to religious orthodoxy or intolerance. Although they would prefer that children live in two-parent families, they also emphasize the need for parental involvement in (and societal commitment to providing the means for) effective child rearing, even by single parents—thus steering a middle course between patriarchalists and feminists.

Although movement communitarians have offered many policy prescriptions (e.g, for personal responsibility, for nonlegal remedies to hate speech, against political action committees, for democratic processes), there frequently has been nothing uniquely "communitarian" about them. Few of these prescriptions hang together in any coherent fashion; indeed, the positions taken often seem to rest on little ground other than political fashion. Their positions have shown this ad hoc character, I believe, largely because communitarians have conceived their mission as an ongoing "quest for balances between individuals and groups, rights and responsibilities," in which "the evaluation of what is a proper moral stance will vary according to circumstances of time and place" (Etzioni 1993, 254–55).

The communitarian challenge to liberalism has certainly provoked a key debate in contemporary Anglo-American political theory (Okin 1989a). Nonetheless, communitarians have not successfully articulated an alternative to liberalism (or conservatism, for that matter). Though they rightly focus on moral and political questions of balance, movement communitarians have neglected to articulate the theoretical principles and practical criteria necessary for guiding the balancing act. In defining a responsive community as one reflecting the human needs of its members, communitarians have forgotten that this formulation begs the question of which needs and values are to be given priority. Indeed, these questions of priority (especially in such areas of deep controversy as the abortion debate) are the preeminently *political* questions—the very ones about which we disagree. They are also questions not easily resolved by a communitarian tradition that counters liberal presumptions of individual autonomy and political neutrality with republican preferences for decentralization of power and the formative influences of the community (Rawls 1993; Sandel 1996).

In sum, the communitarian critique has failed to supplant liberalism primarily because communitarianism (insofar as it has articulated both romantic and republican themes) constitutes not an antiliberalism, but a criticism of liberalism from within its own tradition (Frohnen 1996; Rosenblum 1989 and 1994). In a similar vein, Walzer has noted that communitarianism has often appeared as "a consistently intermittent feature of liberal politics and social organization. No liberal success will make it permanently unattractive. At the same time, no communitarian critique, however penetrating, will ever be anything more than an inconstant feature of liberalism" (1990, 6). Nevertheless, despite its failure to develop a full-fledged theoretical alternative, communitarianism has advanced the cause of theoretical modesty and offered a significant reminder that liberalism occasionally "fails to provide what we yearn for most: fraternity, solidarity, harmony, and, most magically, community" (Holmes 1989, 230; cf. Gutmann 1985). Indeed, one recent result of this restless desire for a politics that accepts both individuality and community, both autonomy and order, has been Rawls's own retreat (1985 and 1993) from Kantian constructivism to a liberalism that is political, not metaphysical—a liberalism that just happens to be constituted by the traditions and political culture of a particular historical community.

FEMINISM

There is more than a little irony in a recent observation that though we are in "a moment when most political theorists have situated themselves more firmly in the liberal tradition," we nonetheless find that liberalism itself has been "extensively criticized for erasing diversity and difference" (Phillips 1994, 74). This paradoxical result may be traced to the fact that most of the ideologies we have discussed have developed both within and outside liberalism. Feminism has been no exception: "The roots of both doctrines lie in the emergence of individualism as a general theory of social life; neither liberalism nor feminism is conceivable without some conception of individuals as free and equal beings, emancipated from the ascribed, hierarchical bonds of traditional society" (Pateman 1991, 116). Typically, surveys of the varieties of feminist thought have begun with the Enlightenment thought of Mary Wollstonecraft or with the stress on legal and political equality fostered by such organizations as the National Organization for Women and the National Women's Political Caucus (Jaggar 1983; Nye 1988; Tong 1989).

Still, although feminism has been cognizant of its historic links to liberalism, contemporary feminist theorists have been highly critical of many of its concepts and assumptions—primarily because liberalism has been so rooted in masculinist perspectives that, when it speaks of the individual, it

> really means "male individual"; that liberalism fails to live up to its radical claim for equitable treatment; that it misrepresents the relationship between the private and the public by speaking of these as distinct rather than as intertwined spheres; and that, by failing to concern itself with the concrete experiences of everyday life, it ignores important social needs and communal responsibilities. (Farganis 1994, 104)

Despite the frequent use of this critique, the variety of feminist traditions now present makes it impossible to identify anything like a single, unitary feminist viewpoint. Of course, there are some family resemblances among the various strains of feminist theory. Feminists clearly seek to advance women's interests in the context of pervasive discrimination and inequality, and many feminists hold that doing so requires radical or even revolutionary social, economic, and political change (Delmar 1994). Moreover, feminists are surely united by their commitment to change and by the hope of eventual liberation—a stance that doubtless requires "the construction of the consciousness, the imaginative apprehension, of oppression, and so of possibility" (Haraway 1994, 424).

Part of that apprehension of oppression involves the development and presentation of cogent critiques of several aspects of liberal political and social theory. Throughout such a program of "gynocriticism," the aim has been to adopt a "standpoint epistemology" that both recalls and restores value to what has been traditionally neglected—namely, women's experience (Clough 1994; Hartsock 1985; Hirschmann 1989; Showalter 1981). One of the key aspects of liberalism to be criticized from this perspective has been its long-standing reliance upon a distinction between public and private spheres of action. The feminist critique of that distinction notably grew out of a liberal drive for moral and political autonomy. Prominent liberal thinkers like Wollstonecraft (1985) and John Stuart Mill (1971) long ago called for an end to the barriers that limited opportunities for nourishing and nurturing women's reason, and in doing so they criticized such practices and doctrines as the law of coverture. Despite these attacks, though, many early feminist thinkers still believed that giving women greater educational, occupational, or political freedom would usefully prepare them to be better mothers to their children and helpmates to their husbands.

More recent feminist writings (recognizing that "the personal is political") have generally concluded with Carole Pateman that "the dichotomy between the private and the public obscures the subjection of women to men within an apparently universal, egalitarian and individualist order" (1991, 118). By restricting women to the private sphere, men could retain exclusive domain over the affairs of political and economic life. And since public policy, by definition, could not extend its reach to the private realm of hearth and home, men could rule there as well—whether benevolently or abusively. In many ways, so long as it is accepted, the public/private dichotomy remains but one of the many conceptual oppositions that privilege the terms linked with men and their experiences, while denigrating those associated with women: for example, culture/nature, mind/body, reason/feeling, subject/object. As a result of this dualistic orientation to experience, liberalism has consistently been faulted for holding an intrinsically gendered, and hence, patriarchal, worldview.

Feminist critique cannot end with this insight, though. The manifold ways in which liberal theory and practice work to deny women both opportunities and validation cannot merely be recognized and acknowledged, debated and criticized. Rather, the conceptual and linguistic dualisms upon which patriarchy rests must be overcome. For some feminists that task requires "deconstructing" the binary oppositions to reveal their philosophical limitations and to show they generally work to keep women subordinate to men (Scott 1994). Yet, the political strategy of deconstruction has its own limits, insofar as it must work within the context of the predominant ways of thinking. For some feminists, then, the task is to generate a "counterdiscourse" that moves in an altogether different context (Hirschmann 1996). In such a context one might jettison the concept of public and private, with its connotation of strict separation of spheres of action, in favor of the image of a network that highlights "the profusion of spaces and identities and the permeability of boundaries in the personal body and in the body politic" (Haraway 1994, 442).

These considerations suggest that the proper path for feminists may well be to work toward developing "a truly general theory—including men and women equally—grounded in the interrelationship of the individual to collective life, or personal to political life, instead of their separation and opposition" (Pateman 1991, 135). Yet, although some theorists might eye the prize of presenting feminism as *the* alternative to liberalism, others have grown skeptical of, if not become opposed to, such an idea. Time and again, poststructuralist theorists have warned of the dangers of looking for all-encompassing theories or "totalizing narratives." As a result it is not surprising that feminism has returned to its original "task of redefining the political to embrace 'the private, the personal, and the sensual,' and, in a growing theoretical literature, has subjected apparently gender-free categories to severe and challenging critique" (Phillips 1993, 77). Similarly, many feminist thinkers have abandoned abstract theorizing in favor of more concrete examinations of various liberal conceptions—including the ones singled out for critique by communitarian theorists, namely, liberalism's conceptions of the self, justice, and citizenship.

Like the communitarians as well, many feminists have basically adopted a conception of the self as socially constructed and constituted (Frazer and Lacey 1993; cf. Sypnowich 1993). Feminists and communitarians differ, nonetheless, when it comes to the nature of the community that does the constructing and constituting—a community that currently, more often than not, appears as masculinist. Some feminists therefore believe that they face an unpalatable choice between a liberal, disembodied subject and a communitarian, determined subject. One preferable alternative has been the conception of a "discursive subject"—one "that pieces together the elements of subjectivity from the discursive mix that constitutes the linguistic world; it is a subject both constructed and creative" (Hekman 1992, 1113). Poststructuralist and postmodernist writings have suggested that our linguistic world is not univocal but is instead populated by many possible discourses—various ideologies, epistemologies, moralities, sexual orientations, social and gender roles. Although these discourses may constitute us and constrict our life choices, they nonetheless provide the conceptual tools and resources for creating counterdiscourses of resistance and for choosing new courses of life.

This conception of a discursive subject, one characterized by a variety of facets and possible futures, underscores an important aspect of recent theorizing in a feminist vein. Although feminists and communitarians have shared a preoccupation with conceptual critique, feminists generally have pursued a different tack by seeking to expose and undermine the gendered character of both liberal *and* communitarian thinking. The point here is that for us to redeem our theoretical concepts, we need to both *de*gender theory (thus emphasizing the universal applicability of our conceptions) and *en*gender it (thereby highlighting the concrete and specific situations in which they may or may not apply). In other words feminist thinkers must both expose (in order to jettison) the roots of our concepts in masculinist thought and, at the same time, reformulate them so that they more adequately capture relevant aspects of women's experience. That is, in rethinking the categories of political analysis, theorists must now acknowledge the claims of difference as well as those of sameness and equality (Phillips 1993; Jones 1990).

In the context of the concept of justice, Susan Moller Okin's examination (1989b) of liberal and conservative theories serves as a landmark text. Effectively showing the extent to which both communitarian and liberal theories have neglected women's experience, Okin has demonstrated the power of conceptual criticism. In her view the central failure of both liberal and communitarian theories is that they do not take into account the ramifications of the sexual division of labor. The gendered division of labor and power can be found in both the theoretical assumption of a public/private dichotomy and the practical realities of family life. Whereas Rawls merely assumed family life, without investigating its gendered character, his communitarian critics have tended to fall back on a nostalgic idealization of the traditional family. The only solution to these problems is to make liberalism apprehend the family as a political institution and thereby extend standards of justice developed for the public sphere to the private sphere, comprehending the family as a school of justice (Okin 1989a, 47–53, and 1989b, 17–23).

Even so, after dismissing communitarian views, Okin concluded her work by acknowledging the liberatory and egalitarian potential of Rawls's difference principle. It appears that for some theories (e.g., those of Alasdair MacIntyre or Robert Nozick) the flaws of gender exclusivity and sexism are fatally damaging, whereas for others (e.g., those of John Rawls and Michael Walzer) they are not. Aside from her cogent analysis of (and appealing remedies for) the injustice of women's social and political condition, much of what Okin says seems to be derived not only from the salvageable portions of Rawls and Walzer, but also from the very liberal tradition that other feminists have criticized for its neglect of difference (Sypnowich 1993, 494–96). For example, the very principle of justice she advances, although apparently designed to recognize the claims of difference, nevertheless asserts that "public policies and laws should generally assume no social differentiation of the sexes" (Okin 1989b, 175). Indeed, Okin's theory appears as little more than a restated version of the previously rejected, patriarchal view held by Aristotle—that is, that justice demands we treat equals equally and unequals unequally.

While Okin has successfully degendered our thinking about justice, other theorists have sought to follow Carol Gilligan's lead (1982) and advance an engendered alternative to the liberal conception of justice. In contrast with a masculinist "ethic of justice" that emphasizes the claims of universal moral principles rooted in notions of right and fairness, feminists have instead offered a woman-centered "ethic of care" that centers on notions of responsibilities and relationships applied in specific and concrete contexts. Whereas an ethic of justice relies upon a more individualistic and atomistic conception of the self, an ethic of care tends to regard the self as one enmeshed in a web of relationships (Tronto 1987; Flanagan and Jackson 1990; Kymlicka 1990). Though these two ethics are not necessarily incompatible, their philosophical construction has all too often replicated the dichotomy between the public and the private, instead of giving us useful insights into "the political dimensions of the private sphere and the complexity of the politics of identity" (Jones 1990, 800).

Seeking to break the chains of that dichotomy, some feminist theorists have begun to explore the concept of citizenship. The prevailing view of citizenship is, of course, quite well known. Rooted in atomistic individualism, the liberal conception regards citizenship as a matter of equal status and individual rights. Citizenship's historical development involves the progressive recognition that formal rights of political participation and economic activity belong to ever-expanding categories of individuals. Of course, from most feminist standpoints, this approach to understanding citizenship rests upon two pernicious fictions: (1) a classless universalism that, in fact, was premised upon the exclusions of class society, and (2) a distinction between the public and private spheres that effectively privileged a conception of citizenship as "less a collective, political activity than an individual, economic activity—the right to pursue one's interests, without hindrance, in the market-place" (Dietz 1992, 67).

Some alternative conceptions of citizenship are equally inadequate, though. The Marxist idea that true citizenship will come only with the success of the class struggle and collective ownership of the means of production merely postpones the discussion. It never adequately answers the question of how politics is to be conducted after the revolution; indeed, it has no conception of politics within a classless society. In addition, the more recent advent of a maternal feminist approach to citizenship (as well as a similar approach to the theory of justice) has focused on embracing an "ethic of care"—an ethic derived from woman's unique experiences and her sense of connectedness with others. Yet the maternalist view also fails, insofar as its approach commits the all-too-liberal fault of universalizing the historically distinct experience of particular groups of people. Quite simply, not all women are mothers, and not all mothers have the same experience with maternal bonds and roles.

Critical of both Marxist and maternalist approaches to citizenship, Mary Dietz (1992) has advanced an alternative feminist conception that moves beyond liberalism while retaining a few of its strands. Resurrecting civic republicanism, she has put forward a democratic conception of citizenship that "takes politics to be the collective and participatory engagement of citizens in the determination of the affairs of their community" (Dietz 1992, 75). What makes this position feminist enough to be palatable is its stress on positive liberty, participatory self-government, and relations of mutual respect among peers. In short, Dietz's brand of feminism involves going back to the future in order to take citizenship seriously and reclaim valuable democratic principles.

Iris Marion Young (1990) has taken a different approach to undermining the prevailing liberal conception of citizenship. She has asserted that the traditional approach to citizenship is highly problematic, insofar as its stress on universality and inclusiveness was actually premised upon homogeneity and exclusion. The politics of the world in which citizenship first came to be conceived not only thoroughly excluded women, but it also scrupulously avoided confronting the reality of group differentiation (whether by attributes or by identity). As a remedy for these failures, a conception of "differentiated citizenship" would lead us to acknowledge that minority and disadvantaged groups have significant rights to special representation, cultural preservation, and self-government (Kymlicka and Norman 1994, 370–73). Young (1990, 128) thus has argued that a truly democratic society needs to create practices and mechanisms for the effective representation and participation of its constituent groups. In this view, it seems, to be a citizen is to be simultaneously a member of, and a participant in, qualitatively different worlds.

Finally, as Kathleen Jones has discussed, yet a third approach taken by feminists has sought a conception of citizenship that is "at once intimate and political" (1990, 811). Placing the discussion of citizenship in the context of family or friendship, such theorists would regard the citizen not so much from the masculinist standpoint of fraternity or comradeship, but from the feminist vantage point of sisterhood or friendship. In such a context, future relations among citizens would take on the emotional ties and commitments found among idealized kinship and friendship groups—ties that are more intense, continuous, nurturant, and multidimensional. Thus, "affective ties replace functional ones as the cement of a social order, the creative development of personality substitutes for the pursuit of instrumental goals, and a shared sense of community takes the place of the competitive norms of capitalist culture" (Jones 1990, 807).

Like the communitarian critique, the feminist examination of key liberal conceptions has come full circle. Feminists began by acknowledging that the social processes that construct our lives have produced rather different experiences for men and women. Further, these differences have been both embodied and hypostatized in a distinction between the public and private spheres. The path to emancipation for women has therefore been through arguments that reveal the arbitrary and self-perpetuating nature of that distinction and its associated conceptions of the self, justice, and citizenship. But in seeking to render that distinction and those conceptions arbitrary, there is a tendency to proclaim that "context is all"—privileging the presumed virtues of the private sphere (as currently conceived) over those of the public and thereby reinstating the very distinction one sought to overthrow.

As a means to ideological change, then, the path of conceptual critique appears to be a limited one. Conceiving its task as presenting alternative theoretical conceptions that transcend the errors of liberalism and communitarianism, feminism concludes by arguing for both individuality and community, equality and difference, abstract impartiality and concrete specificity. In doing so it abandons its position beyond liberalism and communitarianism and instead moves closer to "a more complex and balanced appreciation of the relationship" between the poles of several theoretical oppositions. The force and insight of feminist arguments (especially those regarding the self, justice, and citizenship) have rested largely with revealing the "limitations of previous thought, that exaggerated emphasis on what now emerges as only one part of the whole" (Phillips 1993, 67). Rather than overcoming oppositions, then, feminism as conceptual critique merely reminds us of the rest of the story.

LIMITS OF A SEARCH FOR COMMON GROUND

The Politics of Community, by Frazer and Lacey (1993), illustrates my point about the limits of conceptual critique. In that work Frazer and Lacey set the controversies between liberals and communitarians against the backdrop of the problems of modernity. Each position in this academic "debate"—whether the "welfarist" impulse of liberals like Rawls (staying with liberalism) or the "romantic" impulse of communitarians like MacIntyre (rejecting liberalism and opting for tradition)— has emerged as a particular type of response to those problems. Frazer and Lacey's feminist critique of these responses, though, tries to show how both positions have been inadequate either in comprehending the realities of women's oppression or in providing a useful framework for political theory. The hoped-for result is to identify a compelling theoretical alternative to both liberalism and communitarianism.

As a political theory, liberalism has had a great many faults, most of which have been known and studied for quite some time. One such theoretical failing of liberalism—its assumption of an autonomous agent or a disembodied self—has developed a unique character. This particular model of human life not only has pervaded much of liberal thought, but it also emerged historically as one of the founding ideas of the liberal tradition. If one accepts (for the sake of argument) the validity of social constructionism and the social determination of knowledge, one is left with the paradoxical conclusion that "if liberalism is true as a social theory, this is only because it is, in a wider sense, false" (Frazer and Lacey 1993, 57). In other words, the very existence of liberalism denies its ontological assumptions.

Moreover, despite recent moves by liberal theorists to acknowledge the social, liberalism has failed because it cannot conceive of political life in general, or of women's oppression in particular, in other than individualistic and legalistic terms. (For example, it cannot help but treat sexual harassment as merely another form of discrimination.) Frazer and Lacey have also attacked liberalism by highlighting the ontological and political limitations of contract theory, as well as the problematic distinction between the public and private spheres. Since "the progressive potential of liberalism has been exhausted," many feminists have found communitarianism to be an attractive alternative to liberalism—primarily because both views share an "approach to the social construction of human nature and identity [that] leads naturally if not necessarily into both a constructionist approach to political and moral value, and a substantive notion of political value which gives a central place to . . . public goods" (Frazer and Lacey 1993, 78, 109).

However much communitarianism and feminism may share in their critique of liberalism, though, the two perspectives have parted company whenever communitarianism has appeared as a neoromantic celebration of vague, idealized conceptions such as "community," "tradition," the "family," or "fraternity." Indeed, despite its affinities with feminism, the vocabulary used by communitarians has been both theory- and gender-laden. Feminist adoption of a communitarian position would thus risk reproducing the sexism and patriarchy embedded in a given culture and thereby ensuring that women do not attain full membership in the political community. In the end, just as liberalism could not succeed by virtue of its conceptual blindness, so communitarianism must fail because it cannot escape the conservative implications of its concepts.

Like the German Greens who claimed to be neither right nor left, but ahead, Frazer and Lacey preferred not to take sides in the liberal-communitarian debate. Instead, they staked out a position called "dialogic communitarianism," which emphasized universal access to political institutions, relational processes of mutual recognition and identity formation, the importance of ethical and political dialogue amid diversity. Central to their position was a conception of a relational self that "nicely captures our empirical and logical interdependence and the centrality to our identity of our relations with others and with practices and institutions, whilst retaining an idea of human uniqueness and discreteness as central to our sense of ourselves" (Frazer and Lacey 1993, 178). Also key to the position were commitments to an egalitarian conception of citizenship (including the concrete conditions necessary for such citizenship), and to the elimination of oppression through a democratic practice stressing dialogue and participation.

As with the undiluted strains of communitarianism and feminism, this search for common ground has not fully transformed the object of its critique. At best, this common ground critique has shown us the direction we must take in order to overcome ideological and philosophical oppositions. At its most limited, it has merely resurrected dormant aspects within a broadly conceived liberal tradition. In other words the critique has become very much like the object of its criticism.

Toward the end of their book, Frazer and Lacey raise the fundamental question of how critique (and ultimately, liberation) is still possible if we are embedded within the very philosophies, communities, and practices that appear to be oppressive in so many ways. "If feminism [or, indeed, any other challenge to a dominant ideology] is to be a merely 'internal' critique, we need to know much more about where the sources of critical insight emerge within dominant traditions and practices" (Frazer and Lacey 1993, 139). One source of that critical insight can be found in the diversity of communities and the multiplicity of discourses characteristic of modern (and postmodern) societies. Though existing modes of legitimation perpetuate the status quo, they typically fall short of actually determining the entire course of social history. Further, the conception of a relational (both connected and separate) self also provides people with a subject and an opportunity for critical reflection through the many consciousness-raising techniques employed by feminism and other social movements. In sum: "Both the multiplicity of meaning-generating communities and the openness of social structures lay the groundwork for the development of dissent, struggle and change" (Frazer and Lacey 1993, 202).

FROM CONCEPTUAL CRITIQUE TO IDEOLOGICAL CHANGE

The difficulties of effecting ideological change through cultural transformation inevitably lead some thinkers and activists to search for a third way. If we can neither truly change the culture nor embrace its errors, then perhaps we can mitigate the ill effects of those errors. For those dissatisfied with a "false choice" between comprehensive change or the stasis of the status quo, reform, amelioration, and incrementalism readily become the order of the day. In this context political ideas are alleged to have become "exhausted," and thinkers proclaim the triumph of pragmatism and the end of ideology.

Of course, the polarization and partisanship that accompanies oppositional politics produces a similar result. Here, we often frame the choice as one between the revolutionary embrace of utopian hopes and the traditionalist espousal of familiar verities. Again, for those not wishing to take either side, it seems that the only rational course is to appeal to the middle class on behalf of a middle way. As if unwilling to choose either chocolate or vanilla ice cream, such thinkers opt instead for a political version of fudge ripple.

Not surprisingly, seekers of the third way want to find some common ground between and among disparate points of view. For many, the site of that common ground can be found with the very building blocks of political thought—the concepts (such as liberty and equality, individual and community) that we use to both understand and discuss political life. After all, ideologies may be conceived as "the complex constructs through which specific meanings . . . are imparted to the wide range of political concepts they inevitably employ" (Freeden 1994, 140–41). They are more than that, of course, since they also try to communicate those meanings in ways that inspire and justify political action. The impulse behind conceptual critique seems to be the view that if we can only get the idea right, then we can finally get the world right.

The search for philosophical and political common ground just described is rather reminiscent of the Deweyan focus on problem solving as essential to the lives of both individuals and societies (Ryan 1995, 28). It is also indicative of a third approach to theorizing about ideological change, once again building from a Kuhnian starting point. Generally, the discussion that followed publication of Thomas Kuhn's ideas about scientific revolutions was as significant for its heat as for its light. In the eyes of some philosophers of science, for example, his approach amounted to little more than reducing scientific progress to a matter of mob psychology. As a result, some scholars sought to reclaim a measure of rationality in theory choice. These scholars thus advanced an understanding of theoretical change predicated upon standard scientific criteria, such as the prediction of novel facts or the possession of greater problem-solving capacity (Lakatos 1970; Laudan 1977).

Still other approaches to theorizing about scientific change have stressed continuity and incrementalism, rather than the discontinuity and radical transformation attributed to Kuhn's theory. Arguing against the "revolutionary illusion," Stephen Toulmin reminded us "that paradigm-switches are never as complete as the fully-fledged definition implies; that rival paradigms never really amount to entire alternative world-views; and that intellectual discontinuities on the theoretical level of science conceal underlying continuities at a deeper, methodological level" (1972, 105–6). Not only is scientific change held to be more rational than Kuhn apparently thought, it involves much less change and much more replication; the essential tension is replaced by an essential unity.

Yet, reaffirming the essential unity of an enterprise has unwelcome implications of conservatism, of satisfaction with the status quo. It also overlooks the obvious fact that change does indeed occur. Those building blocks of political thought, our basic conceptions of liberty or equality or democracy, evolve over time; the meanings they once had are no longer the meanings they have today. As one might recall from the discussion of hermeneutics and critical theory in chapter 2, the noted "linguistic turn" in social and political thought has tended to underscore the middle-ground view that both stasis and change, both tradition and innovation, characterize language and discourse in all its forms. The problem is how to conceive the possibility of innovation when our location in the horizon of a tradition seems inescapable.

Given a reappearance of the dilemma of congruence, we should perhaps choose not to view ideological change as a species of paradigm shift, but instead see it as a process of conceptual problem solving. If so, then we can begin by acknowledging that the linguistic aspects of politics frequently involve shared understandings embedded within common practices. How, then, can conceptual innovation in political thought occur? For James Farr the answer is that "conceptual change may be explained in terms of the attempt by political actors to solve speculative or practical problems and to resolve contradictions which their criticism has exposed in their beliefs, actions, and practices" (1989, 36).

This rather Deweyan problem-solving approach to understanding change has an analog in the work of Martin Seliger (1976). Seliger offered a theory that sees ideological change as a process occurring within the ideas advanced by political parties. In this view any given ideology will comprise both a fundamental dimension consisting of moral prescriptions (basic values and goals) at its heart and an operative dimension of technical prescriptions (such as expediency, efficiency, effectiveness, or prudence) surrounding that core (Seliger 1976, 109). An ideology, then, may undergo change in either dimension by adapting to changes in its environment produced by altered social and economic conditions, the unanticipated consequences of political actions, or simply mistaken policy judgments. These adaptations may involve either fine-tuning technical prescriptions to match the ideology's moral core or adjusting the interpretation of basic values to fit what is politically feasible (Seliger 1976, 192–93).

Although change can occur in either dimension of ideology (fundamental or operative), it most often occurs in the latter. This is mainly because the operative dimension is more subject to the stresses and strains of real-world contingencies, and as such it has to be rather flexible—especially if the party is to have any chance of political success. Further, if any party were to give up its core values, it would do so at the cost of forsaking its ideological identity. Just as scientific research programs may be seen as a "hard core" of principles surrounded by a more flexible "protective belt" of theories, so ideologies may be viewed as a core of basic values and concepts somewhat protected by more flexible systems of priority, meaning, and application (Lakatos 1970; Freeden 1994). As a result ideological change normally proceeds in an incremental fashion, so that any operational deviations from fundamental values and goals can be easily and variously explained away. "Systematic ideological reconstruction" is much less likely than "issue-reassessment," Seliger (1976, 260) has observed. Thinkers and activists do not solve an ideology's political and conceptual problems by converting to another set of core values; they simply reinterpret its policy recommendations to accord with new understandings of the ideology's fundamental principles.

Once again, the dilemma of congruence appears as it becomes clear that no amount of issue reassessment can resolve the mounting anomalies and problems facing a dominant orthodoxy. Though calls for fundamental restructuring may far outweigh appeals for minor adjustments, the obvious difficulty of reformulating the hard core of an ideology remains daunting. Mass conversion experiences for adherents of a particular ideology or religion thus are relatively infrequent, and when they do occur, they may be accompanied by violence and oppression. To avoid those ills, and to advance the cause of reason, some advocates of ideological change have taken the route of conceptual critique discussed in this chapter.

In this context one is reminded of the commonplace in philosophical argument that holds that there are two ways of criticizing a position, either from the outside or from within. From the outside, after gaining acceptance of some universal ideal or transhistorical reality, one employs it as a lever to uproot the position altogether. From within, a more nuanced approach seeks to demonstrate that the position under scrutiny is incoherent—either with regard to its central principles (in the case of ideology, Seliger's fundamental dimension of basic values and concepts) or with respect to its intended or unintended consequences (the operative dimension of policy recommendations).

If this dichotomy is accepted, much of what has passed for ideological change certainly has taken the latter approach. Indeed, in the view of many political theorists, this approach of internal or connected criticism is the only one likely to succeed. As Bell's communitarian protagonist expressed the point: "A critic who tries to push beyond the limits of community consciousness cannot generate any politically relevant knowledge; only criticism which resonates with the habits and modes of conduct of the intended audiences can do so" (1993, 65). Of course, we would not be surprised to find that the critiques so produced result in marginal change at best. Since a tradition's critics have to work with the intellectual materials available to them, much of what they proclaim to be new and vital amounts to little more than a sophisticated restatement of the very ideas under attack.

This realization in fact led us to explore, in chapter 4, the opportunities for ideological change found within oppositional politics, in a direct assault upon the dominant public philosophy. As soon as we embark upon this path, though, the contrast between a "politics of ideas" and a "politics of presence" becomes both evident and significant (Phillips 1994). If we accept the parameters of a politics of ideas, then who represents us is immaterial compared to the importance of what that representative stands for. But should we adopt the standpoint of the politics of presence, identity looms much larger, and the *who* of representation matters much more than the *what*.

Nonetheless, in the context of arguments for ideological change, the politics of presence (however challenging to the traditions of orthodoxy) does not necessarily produce a result different from that achieved by the politics of ideas. Instead, the politics of presence faces the very problem encountered by all political and intellectual innovations that are insufficiently congruent with the dominant tradition—they are deemed either grossly unrealistic or wholly unacceptable. Even if an ideological innovation has the requisite level of congruence, it becomes suspected (even, perhaps especially, by its potential adherents) of being insufficiently radical or discontinuous, of being reformist in character.

The upshot seems to be that conceptual critique, as an approach to ideological change, does not offer a clear and unproblematic path either to the transformation of an established public philosophy or to the ultimate liberation of people from the grips of a tainted ideology. More often than not, conceptual critique suffices to lay the groundwork only for further efforts at conceptual critique (Cochran 1989, 432–35). Getting the idea right, then, does not necessarily allow us to get the world right. In this sense, because it begins from where we are and works with the materials at hand, philosophy does indeed leave everything as it is.

THEORIZING
IDEOLOGICAL CHANGE
Subaltern Lessons, Modest Conclusions

6

Ideologies change—perpetually, but with great difficulty. Differences among the manifold strains of public philosophy suggest that ideological change is relatively constant. Yet, when we consider the recent history of American liberalism, we find that substantial change in our political discourse has occurred only once—with the advent of a reform liberalism begun in the Progressive era and institutionalized by the New Deal. Despite the presence of many competitors and numerous critics, this version of liberalism has long remained the dominant orthodoxy.

Doubtless, some of its critics have pessimistically concluded that ideological change is all but impossible. The fact that we are historically embedded in a tradition, as the hermeneutic philosophers have reminded us, certainly makes it difficult to find a vantage point from which to transform consciousness. The vague, all-encompassing nature of the American Creed means that when we are called to think about or act within American politics, when we are interpellated as political subjects in this culture, we all too quickly find that there is no outside position from which to criticize prevailing ways of looking at the world. Should we try to oppose the dominant tradition in a more straightforward and defiant way, we soon recognize that we must remain within familiar realms of discourse, if we expect to be politically effective. Even the fiercest opponents of an orthodoxy must use its conceptual and cultural materials in order to construct a meaningful and acceptable alternative. Needless to say, much the same result ensues when people seek to transform an ideology through conceptual critique.

How, then, to escape this pessimism, born of the dilemma of congruence? Is fundamental political change possible? For many advocates of change, of course, its possibility is taken as a matter of faith. Otherwise, the integrity and worth of their projects would be called into question. Still, we find it difficult to say more than that the process of change is indeterminate, that it is "only *particular* conditions, converging in a *particular* way, that have the effect of nudging *certain* people in *specific* directions" (Dolbeare 1974, 119–20, original emphasis). Indeterminacy puts yet another barrier in the way of our conceiving, much less directing, successful efforts at ideological change.

Perhaps there is another route through the maze, though. Consider William Dowling's observation that in our usual approach to reading a text, "we 'hear' only one voice because a hegemonic ideology suppresses or marginalizes all antagonistic" ones, but should we embark on a more symptomatic reading, we would find that "the hegemonic discourse remains locked into a dialogue with the discourse it has suppressed" (1984, 131). Beneath every text is a subtext; behind every presence, an absence. As we seek to understand what is said, we must also pay attention to what is not said.

All the same, we have to take care not to step onto the slippery slope of what Paul Ricoeur (1986) called "the hermeneutics of suspicion." Surely, an endless round of mutual debunking of one another's ideologies is a less than fruitful path, and one we should definitely avoid. To avoid it, though, requires that we not simply attack an orthodoxy for its distortions or its incompleteness, but rather demonstrate how its distortions or its incompleteness is not only systematic in character, but harmfully so. This has been the insight behind much feminist criticism of conventional thinking and practice in social and political, as well as academic, life. The standpoint epistemology now in vogue among feminists, poststructuralists, and "subaltern" theorists certainly suggests that one remaining vantage point for a thorough critique of the dominant discourse lies with any discourse that heretofore has been marginalized or suppressed (Collins 1990; Dolbeare 1974; hooks 1984).

SUBALTERN LESSONS

Obviously, given the history of American politics, it does not take extraordinary effort to locate such a discursive vantage point. Nowhere does the gap between America's liberal ideals and its political institutions appear more evident or more poignant than in the treatment and condition of African Americans. A study of minority consciousness may thus illuminate for us the means by which a dominant ideology can indeed be challenged and changed. In the subaltern discourse about race and racism, there may be valuable lessons for those seeking to alter our public philosophy.

In the aftermath of any number of events in recent American history, social commentators, journalists, and ordinary people have often been called upon to reflect upon the meaning and influence of race in American life. Publicly expressed thoughts generally repeat the same tired pattern: white folks start the conversation by stating that American society should no longer be viewed critically, because all this progress has been made—in politics, in the mass media, in educational and occupational opportunities. How can it be, they seem to ask, that we are still racist after all these years? Blacks respond by noting that, although some progress may have indeed occurred, tangible evidence of it has still not been dispersed throughout the African American community. Besides, there is certainly tangible evidence of discrimination—in such mundane spheres of life as buying or renting housing, shopping for certain goods in certain stores, or hailing a cab on a city street. After these polar positions are staked out, a social scientist or a journalist volunteers the considered judgment that, for all the government action we have taken, and despite the warnings given by the Kerner Commission, we have indeed become two nations, separate and unequal.

Throughout this so-called conversation, no one mentions a word about the strategic issues underlying it. We have few, if any, statements about what would constitute real progress in race relations, about how we would recognize progress when it in fact occurred. Apparently, as in the famous remark about obscenity, we would just know it when we see it. Nor, for that matter, do we get much discussion of the various obstacles—political, economic, social, cultural, educational, and so forth—in the way of effective change. Our separate societies certainly cannot hope to become one, cannot aspire to become a beloved community, until we more consciously and conscientiously confront the beasts that block our path.

Repeatedly, thinking people have to confront not only the very evident limits of political and legal reform, but also the more subtle limits of conventional discourses about race. Indeed, both sets of limits have become the focus of what some have called "critical race theory." In this realm of contemporary thought, African Americans and others have pondered the sobering implications of affirmative action as a path to success for middle-class individuals; of a political process that now guarantees a formal right to vote but erects barriers to substantive representation; and of an economic system promising equal opportunity that yields increasing disparities of income, wealth, and opportunity itself. The task for thinkers here is to provide what Henry Louis Gates, Jr., observes is "something we don't yet have: a way of speaking about black poverty that doesn't falsify the reality of black advancement; a way of speaking about black advancement that doesn't distort the enduring realities of black poverty" (Gates and West 1996, 38).

In other words, the goal is to identify a path (if not *the* path) to effective freedom and more equality. There have, of course, been a number of paths already announced and explored; they have ranged greatly—from the bootstrap philosophy of Booker T. Washington to the emigration movement of Marcus Garvey; from the beloved community rooted in the nonviolent resistance of Martin Luther King, Jr., to the nationalist goals achieved by any means necessary favored by Malcolm X. All too often, the choice is posed in a Manichean, dichotomous fashion; one must choose either integration or nationalism, either assimilation or separatism, either Martin or Malcolm. A more reasonable view has instead suggested that the political struggles of blacks are best seen as having occurred in three phases: the struggle for emancipation from slavery, a struggle to gain the status and rights of citizenship, and a struggle for independent space and self-development (Gilroy 1993, 122).

The current task for African Americans, then, is to figure out how to wage the struggle for self-development, that is, to identify and maintain "a contextualized, specified world view that reflects the experience of Blacks" (Crenshaw 1988, 1349). The struggle has (somewhat paradoxically) become more difficult since the American version of apartheid, legally mandated and enforced segregation, was dismantled. The separate space necessary for nurturing such a worldview now has to be created more by force of will than by force of law, and even though it was more present during the 1960s, that period's "politicization and transformation of black consciousness did not become an ongoing revolutionary practice in black life" (hooks 1995, 192).

Efforts at consciousness change thus continue to be the order of the day, as they long have been: challenging and resisting the controlling images put forward by white society have made up much of the African American experience (Collins 1990). The hope is that exploring and preserving an authentic, subaltern perspective will reveal what next is to be done, especially now that progress in race relations appears to have been largely a mirage. If racism is a persistent fact of American life, if white supremacist ideas do indeed have a symbiotic relationship with liberal democratic ones, the question of how to effect change becomes particularly poignant (Bell 1987 and 1992).

Therefore, the stake in ideological change is as great for African Americans as it is for anyone else, if it is not greater. To the extent that white supremacist ideas—both the root and the legacy of slavery—are tied to the liberal tradition, transforming or overturning that tradition becomes a necessity. "Until this culture can acknowledge the pathology of white supremacy, we will never create a cultural context wherein the madness of white racist hatred of blacks or the uncontrollable rage that surfaces as a response to that madness can be investigated, critically studied, and understood" (hooks 1995, 26). Further, we cannot hope to eliminate or minimize racism and its effects until we significantly alter liberal ideology.

Yet, most African American thinkers who would challenge liberalism have found it difficult to escape the discursive boundaries set by its orthodoxies. Even for those who are most evidently Other in this society, finding a location outside the dominant ideology remains an elusive goal. One contemporary theorist has criticized W. E. B. Du Bois for falling victim to such a constraint by advancing an inadequate worldview with "false dichotomies of expert knowledge vs. mass ignorance, individual autonomy vs. dogmatic authority, and self-mastery vs. intolerant tradition." Rather than these dualisms, as Cornel West further asserts, our tragicomic times "require more democratic concepts of knowledge and leadership which highlight human fallibility and mutual accountability; notions of individuality and contested authority which stress dynamic traditions; and ideals of self-realization within participatory communities" (Gates and West 1996, 64).

In addition to the approaches to ideological change previously discussed, then, subaltern experience puts one more consideration in the hopper. Those who consider the material implications of ideology, its actual impact on political behavior, have to address the question of who is to be the agent of ideological change. For some, the answer is that people in a specific class location (e.g., the proletariat or perhaps a *Lumpenproletariat*) must necessarily carry the new ideology. Others assign intellectuals the tasks of strategy and critique. Still others argue that the answer does not lie in identifying a category of people who collectively shoulder the brunt of transformative efforts, since the agents of ideological change are as much individuals as they are the bearers of role demands. Once we acknowledge the incomplete character of socialization into a social and political order, we can perhaps begin to understand how it is possible for people with democratic commitments to emerge—whether within the relatively free order of the United States or, for that matter, within the more tightly controlled order of the People's Republic of China.

One path for the individual agent of change may well be a "psychic conversion" that calls for "not simply a rejection of the white lenses through which one sees oneself but, more specifically, a refusal to measure one's humanity by appealing to any white supremacist standard" (West 1992, 50; cf. Baraka 1992). Though the precise source of this conversion is not very clear, certainly no individual can fully develop or persist as an agent of ideological change apart from a nurturing community of similarly situated, like-minded people. Still, finding that refuge, drawing strength and courage from life in a space of one's own, does not guarantee success in effecting ideological change. At the same time as it provides the critical distance requisite to ideological transformation, the "double consciousness" induced by separation from the mainstream may well make effective social and political life more difficult (Du Bois 1961; Gilroy 1993).

Not unlike the dilemma of congruence noted earlier, the pervasive double consciousness engendered by subaltern experience readily encourages the potential agent of change to seek some middle ground that avoids the pitfalls and errors of standard alternatives. The path of the third way has been a significant one in the history of modern ideologies, as any number of positions (democratic socialism, Eurocommunism, communitarianism, and libertarianism, among others) have each tried to claim this status from time to time. Searching for a path between two absolute or extreme positions has thus been a major preoccupation for any set of challengers to the status quo, but especially for those who must develop discursive "strategies that draw attention to one's plight . . . without reinscribing a paradigm of victimization" (hooks 1995, 58).

Certainly, the ideological hegemony of white supremacy poses a very difficult problem of just how to bring about any fundamental and lasting transformation of race relations. Despite some isolated and limited gains, neither litigation nor direct action has yet produced this sort of transformation. As a matter of fact, though, none of the other possible strategies (emigration, internal cultural development, voter registration, economic self-development) has had a different effect. African Americans now therefore encounter the dilemma of how to "evolve a new vision for achieving racial justice—one that would not rely on violent revolution nor require a black exodus" (Bell 1987, 100).

Not surprisingly, the middle-ground path does not immediately captivate legions of potential adherents. Although it is attractive to partisans of the very approaches it seeks to transcend, the possibility of such a path seems increasingly remote just as the need for it grows amid highly polarized debate. Still, the ultimate merit of the third way rests in its congruence with the ideological discourse it seeks to undermine, transform, or replace. Even for African Americans engaged in struggle in the context of a lengthy history of "black strivings," the middling path "rests on the vision of this country as a truly democratic society of liberated men and women, all of whom are endowed with dignity and self-respect, and all of whom enjoy equal opportunity unhindered by race, religion, or class discrimination" (Bell 1987, 251).

Just as Ricoeur observed, a utopian vision represents a potent source of motivation for advocates of ideological change. For Derrick Bell, though, one's utopianism must also have an overlay of a stark, pessimistic realism. Our reform efforts bring little more than isolated or occasional "peaks of progress"; they do not usher in the millennium, or anything close to it. But though racism persists and its damaging effects linger, there remains some hope that seemingly hostile policies hold a progressive potential that African Americans can exploit. If we are clever enough to discern that potential, we could conceivably turn setbacks into triumphs. Facing both the eventual failure of struggle and white society's intermittent commitment to change, there is little to do but to remain steadfast in pursuit of the goal—keep one's eyes on the prize. Despite evident problems with this or that path to liberation, blacks today can do no less than their predecessors did when faced with the horrors of slavery: "fashion a philosophy that both matches the unique dangers [they] face, and enables [them] to recognize in those dangers opportunities for committed living and humane service" (Bell 1992, 195).

In crafting such a philosophy, as we have seen in the context of other efforts at ideological change, the dilemma of congruence remains a significant factor. In her review of the ideological sources of legal reform's limited success, Kimberlé Crenshaw (1988) tried to confront the dilemma straightforwardly. Noting that direct challenges to liberal ideology's legitimacy are unlikely to achieve real gains for blacks, she nonetheless acknowledged that liberalism may have some potential to transform social relations, combat exclusion and oppression, and realize important aspirations. As a result, African American thinkers and activists have to be engaged in "a struggle for inclusion, an attempt to manipulate elements of the dominant ideology to transform the experience of domination. It is a struggle to create a new status quo through the ideological and political tools that are available" (Crenshaw 1988, 1386). The question, of course, is how this struggle is to be carried out.

African Americans struggling to modify or replace the dominant liberal tradition have argued their case very much along the lines of the approaches to ideological change discussed above. Cultural transformation has been the path taken by believers in the dream of a beloved community, founded in ideals of equality, justice, and democracy. It has also been the approach of those seeking to end racism (as well as sexism and class inequalities) through the multifocused efforts of a multiracial coalition (Collins 1992; hooks 1995; West 1992 and 1993). In the 1960s, of course, arguments concerning nationalism and separatism were the predominant form taken by oppositional politics, only to be replaced since then by more a diffuse politics of cultural identity and difference. We can also find analogs of conceptual critique in the traditions of legal discourse, critical or otherwise, involved in the development of antidiscrimination and civil rights law—a discourse that has itself been criticized in important respects (Crenshaw 1988; Williams 1991).

Thus, subaltern thinkers and activists appear to have pursued all the paths to ideological change studied in this book, in hopes of unleashing the liberatory potential of liberalism. Yet, as with the New Left and New Right activists, the limits imposed by the dilemma of congruence remind us from time to time that, since ideological change does not come easily, its advocates often settle for little more than what appears to be an authentic expression of cultural identity. Nonetheless, we have to acknowledge that "the inescapability and legitimate value of muta-tion, hybridity, and intermixture" mean that cultural absolutism of whatever stripe is probably not likely to effect significant ideological change (Gilroy 1993, 223). Instead, the complexity produced by varied histories and plural viewpoints suggests that a more fruitful path to change lies in the resurrection of submerged yet vital elements of the dominant tradition and through the revival of interest in the work of somewhat forgotten predecessors. Perhaps as some kind of tribute to the lives and thoughts of those who came before us, it seems that the only philosophy worth having is one that accepts both the proximate necessity and the ultimate futility of political action.

THEORIES OF CHANGE

Before exploring the outlines of this philosophy, let us return to the notes made in previous chapters regarding theories of change in several contexts (social, political, scientific, and conceptual) and try to assess these approaches with respect to their application regarding recent ef-forts at transforming American liberalism. The goal throughout has been to work toward a theory of ideological change, but at this point "theory" may well be a purely honorific title. Much work remains to be done, especially with regard to other ideological traditions and other political cultures, before we will have arrived at a full-fledged theory. At the very least, though, we should be able to offer some modest conclu-sions about the nature of ideological change.

For all the focus on ideology in the social sciences, remarkably few attempts have been made at theorizing explicitly about ideological change. Therefore, we have had to seek guidance from accounts of change in other contexts. Although theories of social, political, or scien-tific change are many, we can nonetheless identify some general types of theories based partly on the kind of change postulated (discontinuous or incremental) and partly on the type of mechanism that brings change about (sociological or philosophical). I do not intend the list of theories presented here to be exhaustive, nor am I ready to offer a sys-tematic discussion of the types and their respective positions on certain dimensions of variation. All I want to do at this point is to illustrate some of the considerations one must take into account in order to un-derstand the phenomenon of ideological change.

The first type of transformative theory we encountered, when we considered arguments for cultural transformation, focuses on the notion of paradigm shifts and related concepts. The enormity of the task of bringing about a fundamental reconstruction of a dominant public philosophy certainly made the view of scientific change as the rise and fall of paradigms seem an attractive model. But, as we later discovered, the model's attractiveness had to be qualified somewhat. Though the paradigm-shift view assumed that change involved the wholesale replacement of one more or less unitary outlook with another, two important caveats had to be understood: first, that a difficult dilemma of congruence faces any advocate of ideological change through a cultural Gestalt switch, and second, that ideological traditions such as liberalism are more multivocal than they may first appear.

After considering arguments derived from a stance of oppositional politics, it became clear that, in some respects, the prospects for transforming a public philosophy depend upon reviving submerged or even marginalized elements of the dominant tradition. Ideological change is thus less a matter of replacement and more a matter of remembrance. Consideration of subaltern arguments for ideological change has led to a similar conclusion. A project of reviving submerged traditions helps foster both the common identity and the supportive community necessary for people to work together for political change. Moreover, the very task of seeking forgotten, yet potentially subversive, elements of mainstream discourse enables advocates of change to locate the "relevant predecessors" whose life and work can be emulated and extended (Cumming 1969).

Of course, in relying on memory, even thinkers and activists among the most oppositional or marginalized groups in society must at least partially embrace the philosophical foundations of the very ideology they wish to overthrow. The path that remains is to argue for new understandings of the basic values and concepts of the dominant discourse. By working on first principles and fundamental conceptions, one either adapts the prevailing outlook to fit new realities in politics, society, and economics, or moves to an altogether more comprehensive and compelling outlook. In this view, ideological change becomes a matter of conceptual critique and philosophical problem solving. The persistence of the dilemma of congruence throughout these conceptions of ideological change, nevertheless, has left all of them wanting in one respect or another.

Notably, Piotr Sztompka (1993) has recently come to a similar conclusion regarding what he saw as the four basic theories of social change. In his account evolutionary theories emphasize the unfolding of progressive differentiation; developmentalist theories stress a uniform process of modernization; cyclical theories highlight a pattern of either recurrence and repetition or exhaustion and natality; and finally, dialectical theories see historical progress as the result of either natural, impersonal forces or the cumulative effect of human actions over time. Since each theory has its problematic features, Sztompka could not wholeheartedly endorse any of them. Instead, he settled upon a "theory of social becoming" that views society as a dynamic, fluid network of relations in which people create social institutions and practices only in the context of given structural conditions.

Looking at the process of ideological change from this vantage point, we can only conclude that it is necessarily a complex, multidimensional matter. Like more general processes of social change, it must be seen as "a confluence of multiple processes with various vectors, partly overlapping, partly convergent and partly divergent, mutually supportive or destructive" (Sztompka 1993, 211). Clearly, then, some kind of factor explanation for ideological change is most suitable; but which kind? The survey given here of the vicissitudes of recent American liberalism, I believe, points toward an evolutionary account as the most useful model for theorizing about ideological change.

One effort along these lines employed a "population ecology" model to underscore the important role played by random variation within, and competition among, existing religious worldviews or ideologies. Robert Wuthnow (1987, 151) thus saw ideological change as a dynamic sequence consisting of three phases—production (the appearance of ideological variations), selection (a period of competition among those variations), and institutionalization (the successful adoption of one of the variations, as well as its subsequent adaptation to the social and political environment). As with Kuhnian accounts of change, ideologies in this view emerge when there are significant disturbances in social relations or persistent uncertainties about the moral order. New variants appear when the old ones are no longer serviceable, that is, when they no longer provide adequate accounts of our experience. In the face of competition, then, some ideologies will disappear and others will survive, with the survivors being those capable of adapting sufficiently to maintain their relative viability.

In a more overtly political context, a similar effort to theorize about policymaking processes found that public policy tends to emerge from chance combinations occurring among separate streams of policy ideas and political situations. Thus, "the key to understanding agenda and policy change" lies with what happens when the streams come together:

> A problem is recognized, a solution is available, the political climate makes the time right for change, and the constraints do not prohibit action. Advocates develop their proposals and then wait for problems to come along to which they can attach their solutions, or for a development in the political stream . . . that makes their proposals more likely to be adopted. (Kingdon 1984, 93–94)

Based upon the usefulness of this "garbage can" model in explaining aspects of the policymaking process, John Kingdon has also argued that evolutionary models have several advantages in theorizing more generally about social and political change.

First, since evolutionary models are nondeterministic and probabilistic, they can acknowledge the complexity and fluidity inherent in political, social, and cultural processes. Second, because they do not necessarily assume the existence of equilibria, such models can comprehend a variety of phenomena—sudden and dramatic change and nearly imperceptible, gradual change, as well as a certain degree of order. Finally, such models avoid positing either innovation or mutation as the primary source of change. Instead, by focusing on recombination, an evolutionary model "solves the puzzle presented by sudden and substantial change occurring when there is 'no new thing under the sun.' Change is there, but it is the recombination of familiar elements" (Kingdon 1994, 219).

As this analysis suggests, ideologies are likely to be shaped by preexisting traditions that have addressed, in one way or another, the many quandaries of political life. A public philosophy is therefore characterized by a fairly constant pool of ideas ready to serve both as indicators of and as solutions to social problems. The diversity of views found in this pool is at least partly due to the multivocality of most discourses and cultures. Moreover, this diversity may also be traced to the uncertainty that emerges when the moral order is disrupted, or alternatively, when the ideological orthodoxy is undermined or challenged.

Just as obviously, the theorists and polemicists who articulate more or less explicit ideological positions play a role akin to that played by policy entrepreneurs. The social classes or movements that embrace or carry those ideologies serve a similar function. Further, only in certain situations can a window of opportunity open just enough for a dominant ideological tradition to be challenged and, perhaps, supplanted. Though Kingdon's approach suggests that such windows of opportunity may open with some frequency, Wuthnow's analysis argues that it occurs more rarely. Nonetheless, the multivocality of both policy and ideological discourses leads us to believe that competing ideological elements are ever present. They do not appear only with disturbances in the moral order (disappearing when a social consensus returns), but instead remain as continual reminders of both the incompleteness of domination and the inadequacies of orthodoxy.

SOME MODEST CONCLUSIONS

Accepting the insights of both Wuthnow and Kingdon naturally means that we must work to identify the factors most involved in the process of ideological change. Nonetheless, I do not believe that we are at the point where a definitive theory, one that accurately assesses the relative contributions of several factors, can be presented. That would require, as I have suggested, many more detailed investigations of particular ideologies and ideological themes. Still, given the evolutionary framework just discussed and given the limited study of American liberalism presented here, I think that several conclusions about the process of ideological change can now be offered.

First, quite obviously, the fluid and interconnected nature of social and political systems means that *ideological change is significantly related to (but probably not determined by) other types of social and economic change.* It is inconceivable that one could explain the major ideological developments of this century (New Deal liberalism in this country, fascism and communism elsewhere) without reference to technological innovations, to bureaucratic politics and social movements, or to periods of war or economic stagnation. All the same, this does not mean that we can adopt an approach that traces all instances of ideological change to social and economic changes.

Though that reductionist move is not open to us, we should not therefore jump immediately to a more idealist position. The weapon of criticism is a rather blunt instrument, and given the dilemma of congruence, immanent critique certainly has its limitations. It is unlikely that any ideological or cultural innovation will seem all that new and different; instead, efforts to bring about ideological change will likely result in conventional variations on familiar themes, the reinforcement of a dominant discourse rather than its transformation.

Nevertheless, this century's shift from classical to progressive liberalism does at least lend some credence to the idea that ideological change reflects or follows significant social and economic changes. Industrialization, urbanization, the Great Depression, the world wars, and the rise of monopoly capital surely had something to do with the ideological transformation that produced the New Deal in the United States and social democracy elsewhere. Also noteworthy is the occurrence of equally significant social and economic changes in the post–World War II period as well. Chief among these changes is the often-discussed move toward an information- and service-oriented economy, one dominated by the activities and interests of scores of information workers and symbolic analysts (Reich 1992; Toffler 1980; Toffler and Toffler 1995). In the context of a postindustrial economy, capital and its concomitant relations of production and distribution have become increasingly both globalized and centralized. Furthermore, advanced industrial societies have experienced many additional changes—such as the advent of habits of mind rooted in the economics and ethic of consumerism, the shaping of perceptions and meanings by the culture industry, and the growing presence of subaltern populations in both economic and political arenas.

Doubtless, any base/superstructure model that could be supported would require that these kinds of social and economic changes should produce the same type of ideological change that emerged in the first half of this century. For some observers the changes ushering in a postindustrial economy did indeed result in the advent and spread of neoconservatism in both the United States and Germany (Fraser 1993; Habermas 1985). Yet, despite these transformations of social and economic life, no new brand of liberalism has arisen and no fundamental replacement for liberal orthodoxy has successfully emerged. Even though our lives and cultures have been in great flux, the dominant ideology of liberalism has nevertheless been resistant to change. The absence of any such ideological shift is an important clue for understanding ideological change, just as the dog that did not bark was significant to Sherlock Holmes.

It is noteworthy, then, that societies and economies undergo much more momentous and more frequent transformations than does an ideology or public philosophy such as liberalism. Why is this? One explanation might lie with the observation that any new public philosophy, if it is to be accepted, must necessarily mesh with the preexisting one. Stasis and tenacity are thus more likely to mark an ideology and its adherents than change and fickleness. Another possibility is that a reductionist approach to understanding ideological change confronts theoretical and empirical limits of its own. One such limitation can be seen in the fact that the very social and economic changes that have been said to produce neoconservatism and the New Right have also been cited as factors contributing to the rise of neoliberalism, the New Left, and radical feminism. A focus on economic changes alone thus appears to lead to predictions of ideological change in contrary directions; the same set of changes can lead either to the left or to the right. Psychoanalytic explanations of some political phenomena have long faced a similar difficulty, insofar as an ambivalent, love-hate relationship with one's father could turn one into either a fascist or a revolutionary (Adorno et al. 1950; Wolfenstein 1967). Viewing economic changes as key factors in ideological change, then, may well account for the variety of ideological competitors extant at any one time, but such a focus will not necessarily explain why a regnant version of liberalism is or is not replaced by another version.

If we abandon a reductionist approach and focus now on the consequences of conceptual critique, we can come to a second conclusion about the process of ideological change. As I have already observed, both communitarian and feminist efforts to criticize liberal conceptions have led to a number of inconsistencies and self-contradictions. In general, though, philosophical critiques of liberal assumptions and conceptions, from whatever source, have not resulted in the sort of ideological change that occurred earlier in this century. Indeed, such efforts have led either to a muted appreciation of other liberal notions (e.g., equality, mutual respect, dialogue) or to a revival of some presently submerged aspect of the broader liberal tradition. For example, when faced with a rights-based liberalism that emphasizes the protection of individual interests, one could resurrect the communitarian and participatory tradition of civic republicanism, which numbers among its chief advocates such liberal thinkers as John Stuart Mill and John Dewey.

Even so, we could conceive of conceptual change as a more rational process that relies upon widely accepted criteria such as the prediction of novel facts, progressive adjustments in a protective belt of theories surrounding hard-core assumptions, or an improved capacity to solve both empirical and conceptual problems. Nevertheless, absent any external or objective standards, and especially absent any impartial judge, it is difficult to see how competing strains of thought might be evaluated with regard to either their problem-solving or their predictive capacities. Perhaps ideologies could be assessed by how well their policies solve (or predict the courses of alternative solutions to) major social problems, but all too often both the policies and the relevant data are interpreted in inextricably theory-laden ways. At times, it appears, there simply is no ideologically innocent reading either of texts or of social and political life—as Louis Althusser reminded us, there may be no position outside of the dominant ideology.

Perhaps problem solving is better understood in the sense of handling whatever contradictions have been exposed in our beliefs, actions, and practices (Farr 1989, 34–36). Even so, the likelihood of philosophical criticism alone producing significant ideological change is limited, especially if the repeated laments about the alienation of political theory accurately reflect the situation. In any case, it seems that ideological change can be only partly a matter of rational problem solving. More likely than not, the process is more anarchic, more subject to the vicissitudes of fortune, than any analogy to scientific theory choice would suggest. In sum, *ideological change is most likely an incremental and not wholly rational affair.*

If so, are we better off if we conceive of ideological change as a type of irrational, cultural change? As we discussed in chapter 3, the centrality of cultural transformation to the process of ideological change was a noteworthy theme found in the thought of progressives, neoliberals, and neoconservatives. Many schools of thought have recognized that the proper response to an ideological crisis within liberalism may be one that calls not only for changes in public policies, but also for changes in our basic values, attitudes, and culture. John Dewey, for instance, worked as a philosopher and an activist, devoting himself to criticizing the limitations of liberalism, discussing social and economic trends, and articulating cogent ideological alternatives.

The idea of cultural change thus seems like a fairly easy accomplishment, but even in Dewey's case the outcome was not predetermined. This uncertainty makes it difficult to estimate the likelihood of success either for oppositional movements such as the New Left and the New Right or for public intellectuals, whether they are sympathetic or opposed to the dominant orthodoxy. Nor will it help to simply identify ideological change with cultural change, since neither allows us to escape the socially constructed, situated character of our habits of thought. As Alasdair MacIntyre has suggested, although "any theory, any practice, any belief can always under certain conditions be put in question, the practice of putting in question, whether within a tradition or between traditions, itself always requires the context of a tradition" (1980, 63). The implication, of course, is that if we seek to effect ideological change, we lack (more than anything else) a place to stand from which to move the world.

MacIntyre's remark underscores the idea that even when political reformers are at their most utopian, they must still remain fairly pragmatic. That is, *advocates of ideological change inevitably face the dilemma of congruence.* Seeking to replace one ideological perspective with another, they can do so only if the new perspective is somehow congruent with the old. Although transcendence may be possible in the abstract, the limitations imposed by congruence make it all but impossible in concrete settings. Reformers may sincerely and regularly call for cultural change, for new ways of thinking to fit with the new realities society faces, but they also have to work with the ideological materials at hand. As a result, pleas for cultural transformation end as appeals to revived liberal notions of community, civic republicanism, libertarianism, self-development, or Americanism.

Moreover, cultural transformation, as a means to ideological change, is simply too difficult to predict or manage. Societies, polities, and cultures are so hard to steer that any substantive effort to transcend the circle of ideological or cultural alternation is admittedly difficult: "To change a dominant conception of reality requires substantial energy and not inconsiderable initiative. Indeed, this change often does not occur until the gap between what is and what is assumed to be looms so large as to render conventional pronouncements nonsensical" (Reich 1992, 291). Thus, it seems that nothing succeeds like success, and once again, the possibility of directing cultural transformation eludes us. This pessimistic conclusion is shared by Michael Walzer, who has proclaimed that "there is much to be said for a recurrent critique, whose protagonists hope only for small victories, partial incorporations, and when they are rebuffed or dismissed or coopted, fade away for a time only to return" (1990, 6).

What, then, is the key to both understanding and accomplishing ideological change? Unquestionably, there is no magic answer, no royal road to salvation, available to us. Still, a path toward yet one more conclusion about ideological change remains available. It runs through the thickets of culture, tradition, criticism, and possibility.

The dilemma of congruence suggests that agents of change must inevitably hold views rooted (at least in part) within the dominant ideological tradition. This is so because an alternative ideology cannot be accepted unless people see the point of it—that is, unless they can acknowledge its links to familiar habits of thought and unless it somehow speaks to their condition. This is especially the case for political activists who take an oppositional approach to ideological change.

For example, as several scholars have noted, the New Left both consciously and unconsciously rooted itself in several familiar strains of American liberalism. Deweyan pragmatism and the dissident radicalism of C. Wright Mills, as well as egalitarian traditions of civic republicanism and populism, all had their influences upon the early New Left. In similar fashion, neoliberals, neoconservatives, the New Right, communitarians, and feminists have all resurrected many of these same submerged traditions in their simultaneous efforts to "speak American" and to criticize America's deeply rooted liberalism (cf. Young 1996, 340–41).

Our experiences with these efforts at ideological change thus support previous claims about the practice of "connected criticism." For Walzer (1987 and 1988), the connected critic is one who remains a part of the community while criticizing his or her fellow citizens. This stress on the affective ties of the social critic to the community has been criticized for precluding the chance of gaining a critical distance from the critic's own society, and indeed, for preventing the very possibility of effective criticism. Nonetheless, even one of Walzer's detractors has had to acknowledge that the critical task requires that critics (whether individual or collective) interpret and examine social practices in their participants' own idioms (Shapiro 1990, 290–96).

Be that as it may, some thinkers persist in advocating a more transcendent oppositional strategy (Evans 1979; West 1993). For them, remaining within the prevailing idiom should be forsaken in favor of developing a more insurgent body of collective intellectual and practical work that could challenge the social and cultural contradictions found within the established order. Such work would acknowledge the real but not insurmountable obstacles to, as well as the authentic possibilities for, the creation of an alternative society. Yet, despite calling for an insurgent approach, Cornel West has also urged that reformers not forsake the equally important path of "prophetic criticism," in which advocates of change, though "attuned to the best of what the mainstream has to offer—its paradigms, viewpoints and methods," nonetheless retain "a grounding in affirming and enabling subcultures of criticism" (West 1993, 27).

As a means toward ideological change, the practical import of connected or prophetic criticism is that it directs one's attention to political possibility. An explicit focus on possibility recognizes that ideological change will occur not when people try to supplant an orthodoxy with an alternative point of view, but rather "when they interrupt the ideological field and try to transform its meaning by changing or re-articulating its associations" (Hall 1985, 112). Fixing one's gaze on the possibilities inherent in an ideological discourse also means that this rearticulation of associations will highlight unrealized but nonetheless present values—for example, values such as equality, community, self-development, participation, and deliberation. In other words, to focus on possibility is to return to Ricoeur's suggestion that in the very constitution of a text or discourse lies "an original capacity for renewal which is its open character" (1981, 158).

Ideological change thus involves presenting an alternative public philosophy that is simultaneously congruent and transcendent. Such an alternative may be found among the inevitably mixed messages sent by any given ideology (especially in the contrast between myth and reality, ideals and institutions) or within the perspectives offered by a society's multiple and diverse communities (with their subaltern or oppositional perspectives). Primarily, though, *alternative ideologies are found among the varied streams of thought already present within, but submerged or forgotten by, the dominant discourse.*

THE LIMITS AND POSSIBILITIES OF IDEOLOGICAL CHANGE

Nevertheless, the protean character of American liberalism that undermines its hegemony also appears to make it impervious to critique. Michael Foley has likened the American matrix of political ideas to a breccia, the type of conglomerate rock composed of sharp, angular pieces of crystal. As he put it, "America's ideological breccia contains a large number of jagged components which appear to be arbitrarily arranged with no pattern or logical relationship to one another. They

retain their form and separate identities but are nevertheless held together in unison—albeit an unstable and imprecise unison" (1991,
220). What has made this breccia possible, not surprisingly, has been
the unique experiences of American history and the unique yet multifaceted traditions of American political culture.

Finding a path through these interwoven theoretical traditions thus
becomes problematic. Whatever new ideological constellation is put
forward must be congruent with its audience's experience and expectations, else it cannot possibly be accepted. Furthermore, even if one un-
masks assumptions or uncovers the silences of an ideological discourse,
one is "still faced with the challenge of establishing moral authority and
inventing positive values as central elements of any polity." In short,
ideological change agents must develop a "hermeneutic of affirmation"
to supplement a "hermeneutic of suspicion" (Brown 1994, 24).

The conservative implications of these observations are numerous.
Critique, from whatever source, has remained largely an immanent ex-
ercise capable of producing ideological change only at the margins of
liberal thought. As a result it seems that the only remaining option for
advocates of ideological change may well be the sort of pessimism that
sees the status quo as so great and powerful that any transformation in
its doctrines and assumptions is but a chimera. Indeed, an optimistic
sense of the prospects of liberation from the grip of ideology has been
largely replaced by the notion of eternal return, in which critique yields
all the spontaneity of the presidential nominating convention of a major American political party.

Accepting the counsel of the worst-case scenario is certainly one
way of avoiding either surprise or disappointment at the hands of political events. Regardless of our mood, though, it is clear that efforts at
ideological reconstruction have not always been as successful as those
of the progressive liberals. It seems that instances of successful and
wholesale change in any ideological tradition are quite rare. If we are
going to get a handle on the phenomenon of change, then, we should
pay attention to instances of relatively successful change as well as
those of no change at all. As Stephen Toulmin has noted, in the context of theorizing about conceptual change, we need to answer our
"questions in a way that explains, in one and the same set of terms,
both why our ways of thinking in some fields remain effectively unchanged over long periods, and also why in other fields they sometimes change rapidly and drastically" (1972, 122).

In the turbulent times of the latter half of this century, there have been many efforts to criticize, transform, reconstruct, or even supplant American liberalism. Typically, though, the operations of critique tend to flatten the world by reducing all relationships to binary and agonal ones (Gergen 1994). In such relationships alternative voices are usually silenced, and the protagonists engage in a seemingly endless sequence of critique and countercritique, attack and defense. Despite discursive flattening, people within and outside any given debate do have the potential to reproduce and even understand other positions. Immersed in a variety of subcultures, and given access to snippets of political debate through the mass media, most people are familiar with the sketches of alternative positions, if not their fully developed and intelligible arguments.

Because various positions are at least minimally accessible, ideological debate does not have to take the binary course. Instead, one alternative course is for people to adopt an ironic stance that affirms both a position and its contrary, in order to highlight the tentative character of political thought and practice. Another possibility is to create and nurture the capacities and venues for communal, rational dialogue. Both of these efforts bask in the glow of democratic processes. But there is yet another approach to transcending the limits of critique and debate, one in which the protagonists draw upon a set of common cultural traditions.

As I have already noted, thinkers and activists engaged in the process of ideological change are more likely than not to proceed by resurrecting submerged, even marginalized and devalued, elements of the dominant ideological tradition. One important way this is accomplished is through the identification and revival of relevant predecessors whose works reveal alternative yet congruent points of view. Through this and other means, political thinkers and activists not only can remain connected to their communities, but can also foster potentially healthy relationships among the contending parties. A more likely result, though, is a shifting of the ground of debate from current issues and problems to the interpretation and application of a political thinker's ideas.

This simultaneous connection with, and opposition to, the mainstream tradition inherent in processes of ideological change can be represented by any of three metaphors. First, the process of ideological change may be partially captured by Ann Swidler's view that a "culture is not a unified system that pushes action in a consistent direction. Rather, it is more like a 'tool kit' or repertoire . . . from which actors select differing pieces for constructing lines of action" (1986, 277). Faced with the same set of tasks, some agents will opt for the standard set of tools, whereas others will search for special tools that may previously have been overlooked.

Second, the process of ideological change might just as aptly be characterized by Kingdon's "garbage can" model (1984). The materials of ideological change are drawn from continually flowing streams of conceptual critique, oppositional politics, and calls for cultural transformation. Given the right conditions, and an open window of opportunity, submerged or forgotten elements of the main tradition are both resurrected as evaluative standards by which to judge the existing order and revitalized as the utopian cornerstone to a new public philosophy.

Finally, the process of change has an analog in the conception of political theory advanced by Frederick Dolan (1994), a view that highlights the role of the theorist as a storyteller. As an agent of ideological change, the theorist works with the cultural materials available in order to spin his or her particular yarn. Narratives are constructed largely out of an already existing set of texts and themes, as well as a stock of plot devices similar to fairy tales or myths. In this intertextual process, one's contribution to ideological change comes either from retelling the same old stories in different ways or from reviving plot lines and characters from tales long ago forgotten.

In sum, these considerations suggest that a dominant ideological tradition will be relatively slow to change. It simply encompasses too many variants for it to be directly and fundamentally challenged—too many tools in the kit, too many ongoing streams of thought, too many compelling stories. Yet, just as obviously, some of the tools, streams of thought, and stories available for the social and political tasks we face have wittingly or unwittingly been set aside. Significant strains of theory and practice have thus been submerged and forgotten; but when we chance to pick up one or more of them, we begin to see new possibilities for thought and action. Though a predominant ideology can lead to unthinking obedience and mindless conformity, its manifold traditions may be just as likely to provide the means for the creative recombinations of thought that can turn an ideology against itself.

BIBLIOGRAPHY

Abbott, Philip. 1980. *Furious Fancies: American Political Thought in the Post-Liberal Era.* Westport, Conn.: Greenwood.

Abcarian, Gilbert, ed. 1971. *American Political Radicalism.* Waltham, Mass.: Xerox.

Abcarian, Gilbert, and Sherman M. Stanage. 1973. "The Ideology of the Radical Right." In *Political Ideologies,* edited by James A. Gould and Willis H. Truitt. New York: Macmillan.

Adorno, Theodor W., Else Frenkel-Brunswik, Daniel J. Levinson, and R. Nevitt Sanford. 1950. *The Authoritarian Personality.* New York: Norton.

Allswang, John M. 1978. *The New Deal and American Politics.* New York: Wiley.

Althusser, Louis. 1969. *For Marx.* London: Penguin.

———. 1971. *Lenin and Philosophy and Other Essays.* New York: Monthly Review Press.

———. 1972. *Politics and History: Montesquieu, Rousseau, Hegel, and Marx.* London: New Left Books.

———. 1976. *Essays in Self-Criticism.* London: New Left Books.

———. 1990. *Philosophy and the Spontaneous Philosophy of the Scientists and Other Essays.* London: Verso.

Althusser, Louis, and Étienne Balibar. 1970. *Reading Capital.* New York: Pantheon.

Anderson, Charles W. 1990. *Pragmatic Liberalism.* Chicago: University of Chicago Press.

Anderson, Terry H. 1995. *The Movement and the Sixties.* New York: Oxford University Press.

Arblaster, Anthony. 1984. *The Rise and Decline of Western Liberalism.* Oxford: Basil Blackwell.

Arnold, Thurman. 1966. "A Philosophy for Politicians." In *New Deal Thought,* edited by Howard Zinn. Indianapolis: Bobbs-Merrill.

Ashcraft, Richard. 1993. "Liberal Political Theory and Working-Class Radicalism in Nineteenth-Century England." *Political Theory* 21:249–72.

Aughey, Arthur. 1989. "The Moderate Right: The Conservative Tradition in

America and Britain." In *The Nature of the Right: American and European Politics and Political Thought since 1789,* edited by Roger Eatwell and Noël O'Sullivan. Boston: Twayne.

Bailyn, Bernard. 1967. *The Ideological Origins of the American Revolution.* Cambridge: Harvard University Press.

Ball, Terence, and Richard Dagger. 1991. *Political Ideologies and the Democratic Ideal.* New York: HarperCollins.

Baraka, Amiri. 1992. "Malcolm as Ideology." In *Malcolm X: In Our Own Image,* edited by Joe Wood. New York: St. Martin's.

Barber, Benjamin. 1984. *Strong Democracy: Participatory Politics for a New Age.* Berkeley: University of California Press.

———. 1988. *The Conquest of Politics: Liberal Philosophy in Democratic Times.* Princeton, N.J.: Princeton University Press.

Barrett, Michèle. 1991. *The Politics of Truth: From Marx to Foucault.* Stanford, Calif.: Stanford University Press.

Bell, Daniel. 1960. *The End of Ideology: On the Exhaustion of Political Ideas in the Fifties.* New York: Free Press.

———. 1978. *The Cultural Contradictions of Capitalism.* New York: Basic.

———, ed. 1963. *The Radical Right.* New York: Anchor.

Bell, Daniel A. 1993. *Communitarianism and Its Critics.* Oxford: Oxford University Press.

Bell, Derrick. 1987. *And We Are Not Saved: The Elusive Quest for Racial Justice.* New York: Basic.

———. 1992. *Faces at the Bottom of the Well: The Permanence of Racism.* New York: Basic.

Bellah, Robert, Richard Madsen, William M. Sullivan, Ann Swidler, and Steven M. Tipton. 1985. *Habits of the Heart: Individualism and Commitment in American Life.* Berkeley: University of California Press.

———. 1991. *The Good Society.* New York: Vintage.

Berger, Peter, and Thomas Luckmann. 1966. *The Social Construction of Reality: A Treatise in the Sociology of Knowledge.* New York: Anchor.

Bernstein, Michael A. 1989. "Why the Great Depression Was Great: Toward a New Understanding of the Interwar Economic Crisis in the United States." In *The Rise and Fall of the New Deal Order, 1930–1980,* edited by Steve Fraser and Gary Gerstle. Princeton, N.J.: Princeton University Press.

Best, Michael, and William Connolly. 1979. "Politics and Subjects: The Limits of Structural Marxism." *Socialist Review* 9:75–100.

Billig, Mark, Susan Candor, Derek Edwards, Mike Gane, David Middleton, and Alan Radley. 1988. *Ideological Dilemmas: A Social Psychology of Everyday Thinking.* London: Sage.

Biocca, Frank. 1991. Preface to *Television and Political Advertising,* vol. 1, edited by Frank Biocca. Hillsdale, N.J.: Lawrence Erlbaum.

Birnbaum, Norman. 1994. "What Can We Learn from the Movements of 1968?" *Constellations* 1:144–57.

Bloom, Allan. 1987. *The Closing of the American Mind.* New York: Simon and Schuster.

Bluhm, William. 1974. *Ideologies and Attitudes.* Englewood Cliffs, N.J.: Prentice-Hall.

Bohman, James F. 1990. "Communication, Ideology, and Democratic Theory." *American Political Science Review* 84:93–109.

Boorstin, David. 1953. *The Genius of American Politics.* Chicago: University of Chicago Press.

Bordeau, Edward J. 1971. "John Dewey's Ideas about the Great Depression." *Journal of the History of Ideas* 32:67–84.

Bowles, Samuel, and Herbert Gintis. 1986. *Democracy and Capitalism.* New York: Basic.

Brennan, Mary C. 1995. *Turning Right in the Sixties: The Conservative Capture of the GOP.* Chapel Hill: University of North Carolina Press.

Brinkley, Alan. 1989. "The New Deal and the Idea of the State." In *The Rise and Fall of the New Deal Order, 1930–1980,* edited by Steve Fraser and Gary Gerstle. Princeton, N.J.: Princeton University Press.

Brown, Richard Harvey. 1994. "Reconstructing Social Theory after the Postmodern Critique." In *After Postmodernism: Reconstructing Ideology Critique,* edited by Herbert W. Simons and Michael Billig. London: Sage.

Bubner, Rüdiger. 1982. "Habermas's Concept of Critical Theory." In *Habermas: Critical Debates,* edited by John B. Thompson and David Held. Cambridge, Mass.: MIT Press.

Bullert, Gary. 1983. *The Politics of John Dewey.* Buffalo, N.Y.: Prometheus.

Callinicos, Alex. 1976. *Althusser's Marxism.* London: Pluto Press.

Clarke, Paul Barry, ed. 1994. *Citizenship: A Reader.* London: Pluto Press.

Clecak, Peter. 1977. *Crooked Paths: Reflections on Socialism, Conservatism and the Welfare State.* New York: Harper Colophon.

Clough, Patricia Ticineto. 1994. *Feminist Thought: Desire, Power, and Academic Discourse.* Oxford: Blackwell.

Cochran, Clarke E. 1989. "The Thin Theory of Community: The Communitarians and Their Critics." *Political Studies* 37:422–35.

Collier, Peter, and David Horowitz. 1989. *Destructive Generation: Second Thoughts about the Sixties.* New York: Summit.

Collins, Patricia Hill. 1990. *Black Feminist Thought: Knowledge, Consciousness, and the Politics of Empowerment.* New York: Routledge.

———. 1992. "Learning to Think for Ourselves: Malcolm X's Black Nationalism Reconsidered." In *Malcolm X: In Our Own Image,* edited by Joe Wood. New York: St. Martin's.

Crawford, Alan. 1980. *Thunder on the Right.* New York: Pantheon.

Crenshaw, Kimberlé Williams. 1988. "Race, Reform, and Retrenchment: Transformation and Legitimation in Antidiscrimination Law." *Harvard Law Review* 101:1331–87.

Cumming, Robert Denoon. 1969. *Human Nature and History.* 2 vols. Chicago: University of Chicago Press.

Dallmayr, Fred R. 1987. *Critical Encounters: Between Philosophy and Politics.* Notre Dame, Ind.: University of Notre Dame Press.

———. 1989. "Hermeneutics and Deconstruction: Gadamer and Derrida in Dialogue." In *Dialogue and Deconstruction: The Gadamer-Derrida Encounter,* edited by Diane P. Michelfelder and Richard E. Palmer. Albany: State University of New York Press.

Damico, Alfonso. 1978. *Individuality and Community.* Gainesville: University Press of Florida.

Delmar, Rosalind. 1994. "What Is Feminism?" In *Theorizing Feminism: Parallel Trends in the Humanities and Social Sciences,* edited by Anne C. Hermann and Abigail J. Stewart. Boulder: Westview.

Dewey, John. 1930. *Individualism, Old and New.* New York: Minton, Balch.

———. 1939. "The Economic Basis of the New Society." In *Intelligence in the Modern World,* edited by Joseph Ratner. New York: Modern Library.

———. 1946. *Problems of Men.* New York: Philosophical Library.

———. 1954. *The Public and Its Problems.* Athens, Ohio: Swallow.

———. 1960. *On Experience, Nature, and Freedom.* Indianapolis: Bobbs-Merrill.

———. 1963. *Liberalism and Social Action.* New York: Capricorn.

———. 1993. *The Political Writings,* edited by Debra Morris and Ian Shapiro. Indianapolis: Hackett.

Diamond, Sara. 1995. *Roads to Dominion: Right-Wing Movements and Political Power in the United States.* New York: Guilford.

Dietz, Mary. 1992. "Context Is All: Feminism and Theories of Citizenship." In *Dimensions of Radical Democracy,* edited by Chantal Mouffe. London: Verso.

Diggins, John P. 1984. *The Lost Soul of American Politics: Virtue, Self-Interest, and the Foundations of Liberalism.* Chicago: University of Chicago Press.

Dionne, E. J., Jr. 1991. *Why Americans Hate Politics.* New York: Simon and Schuster.

———. 1996. *They Only Look Dead: Why Progressives Will Dominate the Next Political Era.* New York: Simon and Schuster.

Dolan, Frederick M. 1994. *Allegories of America: Narratives, Metaphysics, Politics.* Ithaca, N.Y.: Cornell University Press.

Dolbeare, Kenneth M. 1974. *Political Change in the United States: A Framework for Analysis.* New York: McGraw-Hill.

Dolbeare, Kenneth M., and Patricia Dolbeare. 1976. *American Ideologies: The*

Competing Political Beliefs of the 1970s. 3d ed. Chicago: Rand McNally.

Dolbeare, Kenneth M., and Linda J. Medcalf. 1988. *American Ideologies Today: From Neopolitics to New Ideas.* New York: Random House.

Dorrien, Gary. 1993. *The Neoconservative Mind: Politics, Culture, and the War of Ideology.* Philadelphia: Temple University Press.

Dowling, William. 1984. *Jameson, Althusser, Marx.* Ithaca, N.Y.: Cornell University Press.

Du Bois, W. E. Burghardt. 1961. *The Souls of Black Folk: Essays and Sketches.* Greenwich, Conn.: Fawcett.

Dukakis, Michael, and Rosabeth Moss Kanter. 1988. *Creating the Future.* New York: Summit.

Dunn, Charles W., and J. David Woodard. 1996. *The Conservative Tradition in America.* Lanham, Md.: Rowman and Littlefield.

Dunn, John. 1985. *Rethinking Modern Political Theory.* Cambridge: Cambridge University Press.

Eagleton, Terry. 1991. *Ideology: An Introduction.* London: Verso.

Eatwell, Roger. 1989. "Right or Rights? The Rise of the 'New Right.'" In *The Nature of the Right: American and European Politics and Political Thought Since 1789,* edited by Roger Eatwell and Noël O'Sullivan. Boston: Twayne.

Edsall, Thomas Byrne, with Mary D. Edsall. 1991. *Chain Reaction: The Impact of Race, Rights, and Taxes on American Politics.* New York: Norton.

Eisenstein, Zillah R. 1982. "The Sexual Politics of the New Right: Understanding the 'Crisis of Liberalism' for the 1980s." In *Feminist Theory: A Critique of Ideology,* edited by Nannerl O. Keohane, Michelle Z. Rosaldo, and Barbara C. Gelpi. Chicago: University of Chicago Press.

Elliott, Gregory. 1987. *Althusser: The Detour of Theory.* London: Verso.

Ellis, Richard. 1993. *American Political Cultures.* Oxford: Oxford University Press.

Etzioni, Amitai. 1992. "Communitarian Solutions/What Communitarians Think." *Journal of State Government* 65:9–11.

———. 1993. *The Spirit of Community: Rights, Responsibilities, and the Communitarian Agenda.* New York: Crown.

———. 1996a. "A Modest Communitarian Proposal." *Political Theory* 24:155–71.

———. 1996b. "The Responsive Community: A Communitarian Perspective." *American Sociological Review* 61:1–11.

Evans, Sara. 1979. *Personal Politics: The Roots of Women's Liberation in the Civil Rights Movement and the New Left.* New York: Vintage.

Farganis, Sondra. 1994. "Postmodernism and Feminism." In *Postmodernism and Social Inquiry,* edited by David R. Dickens and Andrea Fontana. New York: Guilford.

Farr, James. 1989. "Understanding Conceptual Change Politically." In *Political Innovation and Conceptual Change,* edited by Terence Ball, James Farr, and Russell L. Hanson. Cambridge: Cambridge University Press.

Ferguson, Thomas. 1989. "Industrial Conflict and the Coming of the New Deal: The Triumph of Multinational Liberalism in America." In *The Rise and Fall of the New Deal Order, 1930–1980,* edited by Steve Fraser and Gary Gerstle. Princeton, N.J.: Princeton University Press.

Fish, Stanley. 1995. *Professional Correctness: Literary Studies and Political Change.* Oxford: Clarendon Press.

Fishkin, James. 1986. "Liberal Theory: Strategies of Reconstruction." In *Liberals on Liberalism,* edited by Alfonso Damico. Totowa, N.J.: Rowman and Littlefield.

Flacks, Richard. 1969. "Is the Great Society Just a Barbecue?" In Teodori 1969.

———. 1988. *Making History: The American Left and the American Mind.* New York: Columbia University Press.

Flanagan, Owen, and Kathryn Jackson. 1990. "Justice, Care, and Gender: The Kohlberg-Gilligan Debate Revisited." In *Feminism and Political Theory,* edited by Cass R. Sunstein. Chicago: University of Chicago Press.

Foley, Michael. 1991. *American Political Ideas: Traditions and Usages.* Manchester, Eng.: Manchester University Press.

Forcey, Charles. 1961. *The Crossroads of Liberalism: Croly, Weyl, Lippmann and the Progressive Era, 1900–1925.* Oxford: Oxford University Press.

Fowler, Robert Booth. 1983. "Does Political Theory Have a Future?" In *What Should Political Theory Be Now?* edited by John S. Nelson. Albany: State University of New York Press.

Francis, Samuel. 1982. "Message from MARs." In Whitaker 1982.

Frankel, Charles. 1977. "John Dewey's Social Philosophy." In *New Studies in the Philosophy of John Dewey,* edited by Steven M. Cahn. Hanover, N.H.: University Press of New England.

Fraser, Nancy. 1993. "Clintonism, Welfare, and the Antisocial Wage: The Emergence of a Neoliberal Political Imaginary." *Rethinking Marxism* 6 (spring): 9–23.

Frazer, Elizabeth, and Nicola Lacey. 1993. *The Politics of Community: A Feminist Critique of the Liberal-Communitarian Debate.* Toronto: University of Toronto Press.

Freeden, Michael. 1994. "Political Concepts and Ideological Morphology." *Journal of Political Philosophy* 2:140–64.

Friedman, Milton. 1962. *Capitalism and Freedom.* Chicago: University of Chicago Press.

Friedman, Milton, and Rose Friedman. 1980. *Free to Choose.* New York: Avon.

Frohnen, Bruce. 1996. *The New Communitarians and the Crisis of Modern Liberalism.* Lawrence: University Press of Kansas.

Frum, David. 1994. *Dead Right.* New York: Basic.

Fukuyama, Francis. 1989. "The End of History?" *National Interest* 16 (summer): 3–18.

Gadamer, Hans-Georg. 1976. *Philosophical Hermeneutics.* Berkeley: University of California Press.

———. 1984. "The Hermeneutics of Suspicion." In *Hermeneutics: Questions and Prospects,* edited by Gary Shapiro and Alan Sica. Amherst: University of Massachusetts Press.

———. 1989a. "Hermeneutics and Logocentrism." In *Dialogue and Deconstruction: The Gadamer-Derrida Encounter,* edited by Diane P. Michelfelder and Richard E. Palmer. Albany: State University of New York Press.

———. 1989b. "The Principle of Effective History." In *The Hermeneutics Reader,* edited by Kurt Mueller-Vollmer. New York: Continuum.

———. 1989c. "Rhetoric, Hermeneutics, and the Critique of Ideology." In *The Hermeneutics Reader,* edited by Kurt Mueller-Vollmer. New York: Continuum.

———. 1989d. "Text and Interpretation." In *Dialogue and Deconstruction: The Gadamer-Derrida Encounter,* edited by Diane P. Michelfelder and Richard E. Palmer. Albany: State University of New York Press.

Gane, Mike. 1983. "On the ISAs Episode." *Economy and Society* 12:431–67.

Gates, Henry Louis, Jr., and Cornel West. 1996. *The Future of the Race.* New York: Knopf.

Geertz, Clifford. 1964. "Ideology as a Cultural System." In *Ideology and Discontent,* edited by David Apter. New York: Free Press.

Geras, Norman. 1972. "Althusser's Marxism: An Account and Assessment." *New Left Review* 71:57–86.

Gergen, Kenneth J. 1994. "The Limits of Pure Critique." In *After Postmodernism: Reconstructing Ideology Critique,* edited by Herbert W. Simons and Michael Billig. London: Sage.

Gerson, Mark. 1996. *The Neoconservative Vision: From the Cold War to the Culture Wars.* Lanham, Md.: Madison.

Gilligan, Carol. 1982. *In a Different Voice.* Cambridge: Harvard University Press.

Gilroy, Paul. 1993. *The Black Atlantic: Modernity and Double Consciousness.* Cambridge: Harvard University Press.

Gingrich, Newt. 1994. "Renewing American Civilization." *Commonsense* 1 (2): 1–15.

———. 1995. *To Renew America.* New York: HarperCollins.

Gingrich, Newt, with David Drake and Marianne Gingrich. 1984. *Window of Opportunity: A Blueprint for the Future.* New York: TOR.

Girvin, Brian. 1988a. "Introduction: Varieties of Conservatism." In *The Transformation of Contemporary Conservatism,* edited by Brian Girvin. London: Sage.

———. 1988b. "The United States: Conservative Politics in a Liberal Society." In *The Transformation of Contemporary Conservatism,* edited by Brian Girvin. London: Sage.

Gitlin, Todd. 1969. "Power and the Myth of Progress." In Teodori 1969.

———. 1987. *The Sixties: Years of Hope, Days of Rage.* New York: Bantam.

———. 1995. *The Twilight of Common Dreams: Why America Is Wracked by Culture Wars.* New York: Metropolitan.

———. 1996. "Straight from the Sixties: What Conservatives Owe the Decade They Hate." *The American Prospect* (May–June): 54–59.

Goldie, Mark. 1989. "Ideology." In *Political Innovation and Conceptual Change,* edited by Terence Ball, James Farr, and Russell L. Hanson. Cambridge: Cambridge University Press.

Goldstone, Jack A. 1991. *Revolution and Rebellion in the Early Modern World.* Berkeley: University of California Press.

Gramsci, Antonio. 1971. *Selections from the Prison Notebooks.* New York: International Publishers.

Griswold, Wendy. 1994. *Cultures and Societies in a Changing World.* Thousand Oaks, Calif.: Pine Forge Press.

Gunnell, John. 1986. *The Alienation of Political Theory.* Amherst: University of Massachusetts Press.

Gutmann, Amy. 1985. "Communitarian Critics of Liberalism." *Philosophy and Public Affairs* 14:308–22.

Habermas, Jürgen. 1971. *Knowledge and Human Interests.* Boston: Beacon Press.

———. 1973. *Theory and Practice.* Boston: Beacon Press.

———. 1975. *Legitimation Crisis.* Boston: Beacon Press.

———. 1984. *The Theory of Communicative Action.* Vol. 1. Boston: Beacon Press.

———. 1985. "Neoconservative Culture Criticism in the United States and West Germany: An Intellectual Movement in Two Political Cultures." In *Habermas and Modernity,* edited by Richard J. Bernstein. Cambridge, Mass.: MIT Press.

———. 1989. "On Hermeneutics' Claim to Universality." In *The Hermeneutics Reader,* edited by Kurt Mueller-Vollmer. New York: Continuum.

Hall, Stuart. 1985. "Signification, Representation, Ideology: Althusser and the Post-Structuralist Debates." *Critical Studies in Mass Communication* 2:91–114.

———. 1996. "The Problem of Ideology: Marxism without Guarantees." In *Stuart Hall: Critical Dialogues in Cultural Studies,* edited by David Morley and Kuan-Hsing Chen. London: Routledge.

Hamby, Alonzo L. 1992. *Liberalism and Its Challengers: From F. D. R. to Bush.* 2d ed. New York: Oxford University Press.

Haraway, Donna. 1994. "A Cyborg Manifesto: Science, Technology, and Socialist-Feminism in the Late Twentieth Century." In *Theorizing Feminism: Parallel Trends in the Humanities and Social Sciences,* edited by Anne C. Hermann and Abigail J. Stewart. Boulder: Westview.

Harbour, William R. 1982. *The Foundations of Conservative Thought: An Anglo-American Tradition in Perspective.* Notre Dame, Ind.: University of Notre Dame Press.

Hart, Gary. 1983. *A New Democracy.* New York: Quill.

———. 1996. *The Patriot: An Exhortation to Liberate America from the Barbarians.* New York: Free Press.

Hartsock, Nancy C. M. 1985. *Money, Sex, and Power: Toward a Feminist Historical Materialism.* Boston: Northeastern University Press.

———. 1991. "Louis Althusser's Structuralist Marxism: Political Clarity and Theoretical Distortions." *Rethinking Marxism* 4 (winter): 10–40.

Hartz, Louis. 1955. *The Liberal Tradition in America.* New York: Harcourt.

Haug, Frigga. 1983. "The Women's Question and the Class Question." In *Rethinking Ideology: A Marxist Debate,* edited by Sakari Hänninen and Leena Paldán. New York: International General.

Hegel, Georg W. F. 1967. *Philosophy of Right.* Oxford: Oxford University Press.

Hekman, Susan. 1992. "The Embodiment of the Subject: Feminism and the Communitarian Critique of Liberalism." *Journal of Politics* 54:1098–119.

Herson, Lawrence J. R. 1984. *The Politics of Ideas: Political Theory and American Public Policy.* Homewood, Ill.: Dorsey.

Himmelstein, Jerome L. 1983. "The New Right." In Leibman and Wuthnow 1983.

Hirschman, Albert O. 1991. *The Rhetoric of Reaction: Perversity, Futility, Jeopardy.* Cambridge: Belknap Press of Harvard University Press.

Hirschmann, Nancy J. 1989. "Freedom, Recognition, and Obligation: A Feminist Approach to Political Theory." *American Political Science Review* 83:1227–44.

———. 1996. "Toward a Feminist Theory of Freedom." *Political Theory* 24:46–67.

Hirst, Paul. 1976. "Althusser and the Theory of Ideology." *Economy and Society* 5:385–412.

Holmes, Stephen. 1989. "The Permanent Structure of Antiliberal Thought." In *Liberalism and the Moral Life,* edited by Nancy Rosenblum. Cambridge: Harvard University Press.

hooks, bell. 1984. *Feminist Theory: From Margin to Center.* Boston: South End Press.

———. 1995. *Killing Rage: Ending Racism.* New York: Henry Holt.

Hoy, David. 1985. "Jacques Derrida." In *The Return of Grand Theory in the*

Human Sciences, edited by Quentin Skinner. Cambridge: Cambridge University Press.

Huntington, Samuel P. 1957. "Conservatism as an Ideology." *American Political Science Review* 51:454–73.

———. 1981. *American Politics: The Promise of Disharmony.* Cambridge: Belknap Press of Harvard University Press.

Isserman, Maurice, and Michael Kazin. 1989. "The Failure and Success of the New Radicalism." In *The Rise and Fall of the New Deal Order, 1930–1980,* edited by Steve Fraser and Gary Gerstle. Princeton, N.J.: Princeton University Press.

Jacoby, Russell. 1994. *Dogmatic Wisdom: How the Culture Wars Divert Education and Distract America.* New York: Doubleday.

Jaggar, Alison M. 1983. *Feminist Politics and Human Nature.* Totowa, N.J.: Rowman and Allanheld.

James, Susan. 1985. "Louis Althusser." In *The Return of Grand Theory in the Human Sciences,* edited by Quentin Skinner. Cambridge: Cambridge University Press.

Jamison, Andrew, and Ron Eyerman. 1994. *Seeds of the Sixties.* Berkeley: University of California Press.

Jones, Kathleen B. 1990. "Citizenship in a Woman-Friendly Polity." *Signs* 15:781–812.

Katsiaficas, George. 1987. *The Imagination of the New Left: A Global Analysis of 1968.* Boston: South End Press.

Kaufman-Osborn, Timothy. 1984. "John Dewey and the Liberal Science of Community." *Journal of Politics* 46:1142–65.

Keane, John. 1983. "Democracy and the Theory of Ideology." *Canadian Journal of Political and Social Theory* 7:5–17.

Keniston, Kenneth. 1968. *Young Radicals.* New York: Harcourt Brace and World.

Kingdon, John. 1984. *Agendas, Alternatives, and Public Policies.* Boston: Little, Brown.

———. 1994. "Agendas, Ideas, and Policy Change." In *New Perspectives on American Politics,* edited by Lawrence C. Dodd and Calvin Jillson. Washington, D.C.: CQ Press.

Kirk, Russell, ed. 1982. *The Portable Conservative Reader.* New York: Penguin.

Kress, Paul. 1983. "Political Theorizing in the Late Twentieth Century: Foci, Loci, and Agendas." In *What Should Political Theory Be Now?* edited by John S. Nelson. Albany: State University of New York Press.

Kristol, Irving. 1976. "What Is a Neo-Conservative?" *Newsweek,* Jan. 19, 87.

———. 1978. *Two Cheers for Capitalism.* New York: Basic.

———. 1983. *Reflections of a Neoconservative: Looking Back, Looking Ahead.* New York: Basic.

———. 1995. *Neoconservatism: The Autobiography of an Idea.* New York: Free Press.

Kuhn, Thomas. 1970. *The Structure of Scientific Revolutions.* 2d ed., enlarged. Chicago: University of Chicago Press.

Kymlicka, Will. 1989. *Liberalism, Community and Culture.* Oxford: Clarendon Press.

———. 1990. *Contemporary Political Philosophy: An Introduction.* Oxford: Clarendon Press.

Kymlicka, Will, and Wayne Norman. 1994. "Return of the Citizen: A Survey of Recent Work on Citizenship Theory." *Ethics* 104:352–81.

Ladd, Everett, Jr. 1978. "The New Class Lines Are Drawn." *Public Opinion* 1:48–53.

Lakatos, Imré. 1970. "Falsification and the Methodology of Scientific Research Programmes." In *Criticism and the Growth of Knowledge,* edited by Imré Lakatos and Alan Musgrave. Cambridge: Cambridge University Press.

Lane, Robert. 1962. *Political Ideology: Why the American Common Man Believes as He Does.* New York: Free Press.

Larrain, Jorge. 1983. *Marxism and Ideology.* Atlantic Highlands, N.J.: Humanities Press.

———. 1996. "Stuart Hall and the Marxist Concept of Ideology." In *Stuart Hall: Critical Dialogues in Cultural Studies,* edited by David Morley and Kuan-Hsing Chen. London: Routledge.

Lasch, Christopher. 1973. "The Disintegration of the New Left." In *Political Ideologies,* edited by James A. Gould and Willis H. Truitt. New York: Macmillan.

Laudan, Larry. 1977. *Progress and Its Problems.* Berkeley: University of California Press.

Leibman, Robert, and Robert Wuthnow, eds. 1983. *The New Christian Right.* New York: Aldine.

Lejeune, Robert, ed. 1972. *Class and Conflict in American Society.* Chicago: Markham.

Leuchtenberg, William. 1958. *The Perils of Prosperity, 1914–1932.* Chicago: University of Chicago Press.

Lind, Michael. 1995. "Why Intellectual Conservatism Died." *Dissent* (winter): 42–47.

Lipset, Seymour Martin. 1963. *Political Man.* Garden City, N.Y.: Anchor.

Lodge, George C. 1975. *The New American Ideology.* New York: New York University Press.

Lowi, Theodore J. 1979. *The End of Liberalism.* 2d ed. New York: Norton.

Lund, William R. 1993. "Communitarian Politics and the Problem of Equality." *Political Research Quarterly* 46:577–600.

Lustig, R. Jeffrey. 1982. *Corporate Liberalism: The Origins of Modern American*

Political Theory, 1890–1920. Berkeley: University of California Press.

MacIntyre, Alasdair. 1980. "Epistemological Crises, Dramatic Narrative, and the Philosophy of Science." In *Paradigms and Revolutions,* edited by Gary Gutting. Notre Dame, Ind.: University of Notre Dame Press.

———. 1984. *After Virtue.* 2d ed. Notre Dame, Ind.: University of Notre Dame Press.

———. 1994. "The Privatization of Good: An Inaugural Lecture." In *The Liberalism-Communitarianism Debate: Liberty and Community Values,* edited by C. F. Delaney. Lanham, Md.: Rowman and Littlefield.

Magaziner, Ira C., and Robert B. Reich. 1982. *Minding America's Business: The Decline and Rise of the American Economy.* New York: Harcourt Brace Jovanovich.

Mannheim, Karl. 1936. *Ideology and Utopia.* New York: Harvest.

McLellan, David. 1995. *Ideology.* 2d ed. Minneapolis: University of Minnesota Press.

———, ed. 1977. *Karl Marx: Selected Writings.* Oxford: Oxford University Press.

Mendelson, Jack. 1979. "The Habermas-Gadamer Debate." *New German Critique* 6 (fall): 44–73.

Mill, John Stuart. 1971. *On the Subjection of Women.* Greenwich, Conn.: Fawcett.

Miller, James. 1987. *"Democracy Is in the Streets": From Port Huron to the Siege of Chicago.* New York: Simon and Schuster.

Mongardini, C. 1980. "Ideological Change and Neoliberalism." *International Political Science Review* 1:309–22.

Moody, Thomas. 1994. "Some Comparisons between Liberalism and an Eccentric Communitarianism." In *The Liberalism-Communitarianism Debate: Liberty and Community Values,* edited by C. F. Delaney. Lanham, Md.: Rowman and Littlefield.

Morgan, Edward P. 1991. *The 60s Experience: Hard Lessons about Modern America.* Philadelphia: Temple University Press.

Morone, James A. 1990. *The Democratic Wish: Popular Participation and the Limits of American Government.* New York: Basic.

Nederveen Pieterse, Jan. 1992. "Emancipations, Modern and Postmodern." In *Emancipations, Modern and Postmodern,* edited by Jan Nederveen Pieterse. London: Sage.

"New House Speaker Envisions Cooperation, Cuts, Hard Work." 1994. *Congressional Quarterly Weekly Report* (Nov. 12): 3295–97.

Norris, Christopher. 1991. *Spinoza and the Origins of Modern Critical Theory.* Oxford: Basil Blackwell.

Nye, Andrea. 1988. *Feminist Theory and the Philosophies of Man.* New York: Routledge.

Oglesby, Carl. 1969. "Trapped in a System." In Teodori 1969.

Okin, Susan Moller. 1989a. "Humanist Liberalism." In *Liberalism and the Moral Life,* edited by Nancy Rosenblum. Cambridge: Harvard University Press.

———. 1989b. *Justice, Gender, and the Family.* New York: Basic.

O'Sullivan, Noël. 1989. "The New Right: The Quest for a Civil Philosophy in Europe and America." In *The Nature of the Right: American and European Politics and Political Thought since 1789,* edited by Roger Eatwell and Noël O'Sullivan. Boston: Twayne.

Ottmann, Henning. 1982. "Cognitive Interests and Self-Reflection." In *Habermas: Critical Debates,* edited by John B. Thompson and David Held. Cambridge, Mass.: MIT Press.

Paris, David. 1987. "The 'Theoretical Mystique': Neutrality, Plurality, and the Defense of Liberalism." *American Journal of Political Science* 31:909–39.

Pateman, Carole. 1991. "Feminist Critiques of the Public-Private Dichotomy." In *Contemporary Political Theory,* edited by Philip Pettit. New York: Macmillan.

Pells, Richard H. 1973. *Radical Visions and American Dreams: Culture and Social Thought in the Depression Years.* Middletown, Conn.: Wesleyan University Press.

Pennock, J. Roland. 1990. "Liberalism under Attack." *Political Science Teacher* 3 (1): 6–10.

Peters, Charles. 1983. "A New Politics for America." *Public Welfare* 41:34–40.

Peters, Charles, and Paul Keisling, eds. 1985. *A New Road for America.* Lanham, Md.: Madison.

Phillips, Anne. 1993. *Democracy and Difference.* University Park: Pennsylvania State University Press.

———. 1994. "Dealing with Difference." *Constellations* 1:74–91.

Piven, Frances Fox, and Richard Cloward. 1977. *Poor People's Movements: Why They Succeed, How They Fail.* New York: Pantheon.

Plotke, David. 1996. *Building a Democratic Political Order: Reshaping American Liberalism in the 1930s and 1940s.* Cambridge: Cambridge University Press.

Pocock, J. G. A. 1975. *The Machiavellian Moment: Florentine Political Thought and the Atlantic Republican Tradition.* Princeton, N.J.: Princeton University Press.

Popper, Karl. 1968. *The Logic of Scientific Discovery.* New York: Harper Torchbooks.

Rancière, Jacques. 1974. "On the Theory of Ideology (the Politics of Althusser)." *Radical Philosophy* 7:2–15.

Rawls, John. 1971. *A Theory of Justice.* Cambridge: Harvard University Press.

———. 1985. "Justice as Fairness: Political not Metaphysical." *Philosophy and Public Affairs* 14:223–51.

———. 1993. *Political Liberalism.* New York: Columbia University Press.

Reed, Ralph. 1996. *Active Faith: How Christians Are Changing the Soul of American Politics.* New York: Free Press.

Reich, Robert B. 1983. *The Next American Frontier.* New York: Penguin.

———. 1987. *Tales of a New America: The Anxious Liberal's Guide to the Future.* New York: Vintage.

———. 1989. *The Resurgent Liberal (and Other Unfashionable Prophecies).* New York: Times Books.

———. 1992. *The Work of Nations.* New York: Vintage.

———, ed. 1988. *The Power of Public Ideas.* Cambridge, Mass.: Ballinger.

Reiman, Jeffrey. 1994. "Liberalism and Its Critics." In *The Liberalism-Communitarianism Debate: Liberty and Community Values,* edited by C. F. Delaney. Lanham, Md.: Rowman and Littlefield.

Ricoeur, Paul. 1974a. *The Conflict of Interpretations.* Evanston, Ill.: Northwestern University Press.

———. 1974b. *Political and Social Essays.* Athens: Ohio University Press.

———. 1976. "Ideology and Utopia as Cultural Imagination." *Philosophic Exchange* 2:17–30.

———. 1978. "Can There Be a Scientific Concept of Ideology?" In *Phenomenology and the Social Sciences,* edited by Joseph Bien. The Hague: Martinus Nijhoff.

———. 1981. *Hermeneutics and the Human Sciences.* Cambridge: Cambridge University Press.

———. 1986. *Lectures on Ideology and Utopia.* New York: Columbia University Press.

Roelofs, H. Mark. 1992. *The Poverty of American Politics: A Theoretical Interpretation.* Philadelphia: Temple University Press.

Rosenblum, Nancy. 1987. *Another Liberalism: Romanticism and the Reconstruction of Liberal Thought.* Cambridge: Harvard University Press.

———. 1989. "Pluralism and Self-Defense." In *Liberalism and the Moral Life,* edited by Nancy Rosenblum. Cambridge: Harvard University Press.

———. 1994. "Romantic Communitarianism: Blithedale Romance versus the Custom House." In *The Liberalism-Communitarianism Debate: Liberty and Community Values,* edited by C. F. Delaney. Lanham, Md.: Rowman and Littlefield.

Rothenberg, Randall. 1984. *The Neoliberals.* New York: Simon and Schuster.

Ryan, Alan. 1995. *John Dewey and the High Tide of American Liberalism.* New York: Norton.

Sandel, Michael. 1982. *Liberalism and the Limits of Justice.* Cambridge: Cambridge University Press.

———. 1984. "The Procedural Republic and the Unencumbered Self." *Political Theory* 12:81–96.

———. 1988. "The Political Theory of the Procedural Republic." In Reich 1988.

———. 1996. *Democracy's Discontent: America in Search of a Public Philosophy.* Cambridge: Belknap Press of Harvard University Press.

Sargent, Lyman T. 1972. *New Left Thought.* Homewood, Ill.: Dorsey.

Sartori, Giovanni. 1969. "Politics, Ideology, and Belief Systems." *American Political Science Review* 63:398–411.

Saussure, Ferdinand. 1990. "Signs and Language." In *Culture and Society: Contemporary Debates,* edited by Jeffrey Alexander and Steven Seidman. Cambridge: Cambridge University Press.

Schlesinger, Arthur M., Jr. 1957. *The Crisis of the Old Order, 1919–1933.* Boston: Houghton Mifflin.

Schoolman, Morton. 1987. "The Moral Sentiments of Neoliberalism." *Political Theory* 15:205–24.

Schurmann, Franz. 1983. "Ideology at the Grass Roots." In *Rethinking Liberalism,* edited by Walter Anderson. New York: Avon.

Schutz, Alfred. 1967. *The Phenomenology of the Social World.* Evanston, Ill.: Northwestern University Press.

Schweitzer, David, and James Elden. 1971. "New Left as Right." *Journal of Social Issues* 27:141–66.

Scott, Joan W. 1994. "Deconstructing Equality-versus-Difference: or, The Uses of Poststructuralist Theory for Feminism." In *Theorizing Feminism: Parallel Trends in the Humanities and Social Sciences,* edited by Anne C. Hermann and Abigail J. Stewart. Boulder: Westview.

Seliger, Martin. 1976. *Ideology and Politics.* New York: Free Press.

Selznick, Philip. 1992. *The Moral Commonwealth: Social Theory and the Promise of Community.* Berkeley: University of California Press.

Shapiro, Ian. 1990. *Political Criticism.* Berkeley: University of California Press.

Sholle, David J. 1988. "Critical Studies: From the Theory of Ideology to Power/Knowledge." *Critical Studies in Mass Communication* 5:16–41.

Showalter, Elaine. 1981. "Feminist Criticism in the Wilderness." In *Writing and Sexual Difference,* edited by Elizabeth Abel. Chicago: University of Chicago Press.

Shusterman, Richard. 1994. "Pragmatism and Liberalism between Dewey and Rorty." *Political Theory* 22:391–413.

Simon, Josef. 1989. "Good Will to Understand and the Will to Power: Remarks on an 'Improbable Debate.'" In *Dialogue and Deconstruction: The Gadamer-Derrida Encounter,* edited by Diane P. Michelfelder and Richard E. Palmer. Albany: State University of New York Press.

Smith, Rogers M. 1993. "Beyond Tocqueville, Myrdal, and Hartz: The Multiple Traditions in America." *American Political Science Review* 87:549–66.

Smith, Steven. 1984. *Reading Althusser.* Ithaca, N.Y.: Cornell University Press.

Steigerwald, David. 1995. *The Sixties and the End of Modern America.* New York: St. Martin's.

Steinfels, Peter. 1979. *The Neoconservatives: The Men Who Are Changing America's Politics.* New York: Simon and Schuster.

Students for a Democratic Society. 1987. "Port Huron Statement." In Miller 1987.

Sullivan, William M. 1986. *Reconstructing Public Philosophy.* Berkeley: University of California Press.

Swidler, Ann. 1986. "Culture in Action: Symbols and Strategies." *American Sociological Review* 51:273–86.

Sypnowich, Christine. 1993. "Justice, Community, and the Antinomies of Feminist Theory." *Political Theory* 21:484–506.

Sztompka, Piotr. 1993. *The Sociology of Social Change.* Oxford: Blackwell.

Taylor, Charles. 1967. "Neutrality in Political Science." In *Philosophy, Politics and Society,* edited by Peter Laslett and W. G. Runciman. New York: Barnes and Noble.

———. 1989. "Cross-Purposes: The Liberal-Communitarian Debate." In *Liberalism and the Moral Life,* edited by Nancy Rosenblum. Cambridge: Harvard University Press.

———. 1992. *Multiculturalism and "The Politics of Recognition."* Ed. Amy Gutmann. Princeton, N.J.: Princeton University Press.

Teodori, Massimo, ed. 1969. *The New Left: A Documentary History.* Indianapolis: Bobbs-Merrill.

Terchek, Ronald. 1986. "The Fruits of Success and the Crisis of Liberalism." In *Liberals on Liberalism,* edited by Alfonso Damico. Totowa, N.J.: Rowman and Littlefield.

Therborn, Goran. 1980. *The Ideology of Power and the Power of Ideology.* London: Verso.

Thigpen, Robert, and Lyle Downing. 1987. "Liberalism and the Communitarian Critique." *American Journal of Political Science* 31:637–54.

Thompson, Edward P. 1978. *The Poverty of Theory and Other Essays.* New York: Monthly Review Press.

Thompson, John B. 1984. *Studies in the Theory of Ideology.* Berkeley: University of California Press.

Tilman, Rick. 1984. "Dewey's Liberalism versus Veblen's Radicalism." *Journal of Economic Issues.* 18:745–69.

Tocqueville, Alexis de. 1969. *Democracy in America.* Garden City, N.Y.: Doubleday.

Toffler, Alvin. 1980. *The Third Wave.* New York: Morrow.

Toffler, Alvin, and Heidi Toffler. 1995. *Creating a New Civilization: The Politics of the Third Wave.* Atlanta: Turner.

Tomasky, Michael. 1996. *Left for Dead: The Life, Death and Possible Resurrection of Progressive Politics in America.* New York: Free Press.

Tong, Rosemarie. 1989. *Feminist Thought: A Comprehensive Introduction.* Boulder: Westview.

Toulmin, Stephen. 1961. *Foresight and Understanding.* New York: Harper Torchbooks.

—————. 1972. *Human Understanding.* Princeton, N.J.: Princeton University Press.

Trilling, Lionel. 1957. *The Liberal Imagination.* Garden City, N.Y.: Anchor.

Tronto, Joan. 1987. "'Women's Morality': Beyond Gender Difference to a Theory of Care." *Signs* 12:644–63.

Tsongas, Paul. 1981. *The Road from Here.* New York: Vintage.

Unger, Irwin. 1974. *The Movement.* New York: Dodd, Mead.

Van Dyke, Vernon. 1995. *Ideology and Political Choice: The Search for Freedom, Justice, and Virtue.* Chatham, N.J.: Chatham House.

Viereck, Peter. 1963. "The Philosophical 'New Conservatism' (1962)." In Bell 1963.

Viguerie, Richard. 1980. *The New Right: We're Ready to Lead.* Falls Church, Va.: Viguerie.

Wallach, John. 1987. "Liberals, Communitarians, and the Tasks of Political Theory." *Political Theory* 15:581–611.

Walzer, Michael. 1983a. "On 'Failed Totalitarianism'." In *1984 Revisited,* edited by Irving Howe. New York: Perennial Library.

—————. 1983b. *Spheres of Justice.* New York: Basic.

—————. 1984. "Liberalism and the Art of Separation." *Political Theory* 12:315–30.

—————. 1987. *Interpretation and Social Criticism.* Cambridge: Harvard University Press.

—————. 1988. *The Company of Critics.* New York: Basic.

—————. 1989. "Citizenship." In *Political Innovation and Conceptual Change,* edited by Terence Ball, James Farr, and Russell L. Hanson. Cambridge: Cambridge University Press.

—————. 1990. "The Communitarian Critique of Liberalism." *Political Theory* 18:6–23.

Warren, Donald. 1976. *The Radical Center.* Notre Dame, Ind.: University of Notre Dame Press.

West, Cornel. 1992. "Malcolm X and Black Rage." In *Malcolm X: In Our Own Image,* edited by Joe Wood. New York: St. Martin's.

—————. 1993. *Keeping Faith: Philosophy and Race in America.* New York: Routledge.

Westbrook, Robert B. 1991. *John Dewey and American Democracy.* Ithaca, N.Y.: Cornell University Press.

Westin, Alan. 1971. "Deadly Parallels." In Abcarian 1971.

Whitaker, Robert, ed. 1982. *The New Right Papers.* New York: St. Martin's.

Wilentz, Sean. 1995. "Populism Redux." *Dissent* (spring): 149–53.

Williams, Leonard. 1987. "Ideological Parallels between the New Left and the New Right." *Social Science Journal* 24:317–27.

————. 1993. "Althusser on Ideology: A Reassessment." *New Political Science* (winter): 47–66.

Williams, Patricia J. 1991. *The Alchemy of Race and Rights.* Cambridge: Harvard University Press.

Wilson, Clyde. 1982. "Citizens or Subjects?" In Whitaker 1982.

Wolfenstein, E. Victor. 1967. *The Revolutionary Personality: Lenin, Trotsky, Gandhi.* Princeton, N.J.: Princeton University Press.

Wolin, Sheldon. 1980. "Paradigms and Political Theories." In *Paradigms and Revolutions,* edited by Gary Gutting. Notre Dame, Ind.: University of Notre Dame Press.

Wollstonecraft, Mary. 1985. *A Vindication of the Rights of Woman.* London: Penguin.

Wood, Gordon. 1969. *The Creation of the American Republic: 1776–1787.* New York: Norton.

Woodson, Robert L., Sr. 1994. "A Challenge to Conservatives." *Commonsense* 1 (3): 11–29.

Wuthnow, Robert. 1987. *Meaning and Moral Order: Explorations in Cultural Analysis.* Berkeley: University of California Press.

Young, Iris Marion. 1990. "Polity and Group Difference: A Critique of the Ideal of Universal Citizenship." In *Feminism and Political Theory,* edited by Cass R. Sunstein. Chicago: University of Chicago Press.

Young, James P. 1996. *Reconsidering American Liberalism: The Troubled Odyssey of the Liberal Idea.* Boulder: Westview.

INDEX